STUDENT STUDY GUIDE

Naima Cherie Prince, Ph.D
Santa Fe Community College

MARRIAGES AND FAMILIES
SIXTH EDITION

Nijole V. Benokraitis
University of Baltimore

PEARSON
Prentice Hall

Upper Saddle River, New Jersey 07458

© 2008 by PEARSON EDUCATION, INC.

Upper Saddle River, New Jersey 07458

10 9 8 7 6 5 4 3 2 1

ISBN 0-13-224883-2

Published in the United States of America

CONTENTS

PREFACE

This study guide is designed to accompany **Marriages And Families: Changes, Choices, and Constraints, 6e, by Nijole V. Benokraitis.**

Each chapter in this manual includes chapter objectives, a chapter overview, a pre-test, an application exercise, a crossword puzzle, a post test, a self-assessment exercise and an answer key.

This study guide is intended to help you 1) identify the key points in the text, 2) apply the concepts and terms presented in the book to the "real world," 3) assess your understanding of the material, 4) improve your score on tests and quizzes and 5) increase your understanding of yourself and your own family.

Naima Cherie Prince, Ph.D.
naima.prince@sfcc.edu

THE CHANGING FAMILY

CHAPTER OBJECTIVES

Upon reading Chapter One, students should be able to:

1. Explain the common characteristics of Western marriages and the types of legal marriages in the United States.

2. Discuss the various definitions of the family.

3. Describe the basic functions of the family.

4. Compare and contrast the various forms of family structures and marriage types.

5. Discuss the myths concerning marriage and family.

6. Compare and contrast the three broad perspectives on how family is changing.

7. Explain the major demographic changes in family.

8. Compare and contrast the micro-level and the macro-level perspectives of why families are changing.

9. Explain why a cross-cultural focus is helpful in understanding the American family.

CHAPTER OVERVIEW

Marriage is a socially approved mating relationship that is expected to be stable and enduring. There are three main characteristics of marriage: shared economic responsibility, monogamous sexual activity, and bearing/raising children. In the U.S., marriages are legally defined as ceremonial or non-ceremonial. A **ceremonial marriage** occurs when a couple follows procedures specified by the state or other jurisdiction. A **non-ceremonial or common-law marriage** is established by cohabitation (living together) or consummation (sexual intercourse). In both types of marriage **bigamy** (marrying a second person while still legally married to another person) is prohibited. **Family** is defined as an intimate environment in which two or more people: live together in a committed relationship, see their identity as attached to the group, and share functions and close emotional ties. **Fictive kin** are non-relatives who are accepted as part of the family. The **nuclear family** is made up of a husband, wife, and their biological or adopted children.

There are five important functions for families to fulfill. The first function is **regulation of sexual activity.** This involves setting boundaries on who family members may engage in sexual relations with and under which circumstances sexual relations may occur. The principle of **endogamy** requires that people marry or have sexual relations within a certain group. The principle of **exogamy** requires marrying outside the group. The **incest taboo** forbids sexual relations with close blood relatives. **Procreation**, or bearing children, is the second function of family and is essential for family continuity. The third function of family is socialization. Through **socialization**, children learn the language, knowledge, attitudes, values, skills, and beliefs that are needed to function effectively in society. **Roles** are the obligations and expectations attached to particular situations or positions. **Economic security**, the family's provision of food, shelter, clothing, and other material resources to its members, is the fourth function of family. This function is needed to ensure the family's physical survival. The fifth function is **emotional support**. This includes nurturance, love, and emotional sustenance that members need to be happy, healthy, and secure. The family is a **primary group**, characterized by intimate, long-lasting, face-to-face interaction. Members of a family may also interact with **secondary groups**, which are characterized by impersonal and short-term relationships. Families also place their members within distinct social classes. A **social class** is a category of people who have a similar standing or rank based on wealth, education, power, prestige, and other valued resources.

There are different forms of family. The **family of orientation** is the family that one is raised by or adopted into. The **family of procreation** is the family that one forms by marrying, having, or adopting children. The **extended family** is comprised of two or more generations living together or in adjacent dwellings. Each type of family is a part of a larger **kinship system**, or network of people related by blood, marriage, or adoption. There are also different types of marriages. In **monogamy**, one person is married exclusively to one other person. **Serial monogamy** is having a series of monogamous marriages. In **polygamy**, one person has two or more spouses. There are two types of polygamy: **polygyny** (a man has two or more wives) and **polyandry** (a woman has two or more husbands). Families may also be categorized by residential patterns or where they live. There are three different residential patterns: **patrilocal** (couples live with the husband's family),

matrilocal (couples live with the wife's family), and **neolocal** (couples set up their own residence).

Most Americans believe some myths about marriage and family. Myths can be **functional** (promoting social solidarity within family), **dysfunctional** (disrupting family), or both. There are three broad perspectives on the changing family: (1) the family is deteriorating; (2) the family is changing but not deteriorating; and (3) the family is stronger than ever before.

Birth rates have declined so that women have fewer children, have them closer together and finish raising their children earlier. The average age of the population more than doubled to 36 in 2004. The combination of these factors have resulted in parents experiencing: the **empty nest syndrome** (the departure of grown children from the home) earlier; grandparenthood at a younger age; and prolonged widowhood. Other demographic changes are the increase in **non-family households** (people who live alone or with non-relatives); a decline in the percentage of married couple households; a growing number of single people and cohabitants; an increase in divorce and remarriage rates; a growing number of stepfamilies; a larger number of one-parent families; and more working mothers. With regards to race and ethnicity, the U.S. is the most multicultural society in the world. There are about 150 distinctive ethnic or racial groups in the country. The number of foreign born Americans is on the rise, as is the number of Latinos, African Americans, and Asian Americans. There are different explanations for changes in families. **Micro-level perspectives** focus on individual social interactions in specific settings and commonly assume that people have many choices. **Macro-level perspectives** focus on large-scale patterns that characterize society as a whole. A cross-cultural, global perspective is offered in the textbook because modern U.S. families are diverse; it helps us understand the family practices and customs of other cultures; strengthens competence for the job market; challenges our ideas about U.S. family forms; and helps us to dispose of stereotypes.

PRE-TEST

1. Lenny and Sylvia had blood tests, obtained a license, and were married by a local judge. This couple has a
   a. Ceremonial marriage
   b. Non ceremonial marriage
   c. Common-law marriage

2. Margaret has been married to Larry for the last 30 years. She has never been married to anyone else. Margaret is practicing:
   a. Polygamy

    b. Monogamy

    c. Serial Monogamy

3. Which of the following is true?
    a. The number of ethnic minorities in the U.S. is decreasing
    b. The number of ethnic minorities in the U.S. is increasing
    c. The number of ethnic minorities in the U.S. has not changed.

4. Cuerline has been taught to marry outside her group. She is from Haiti and she hopes to marry an American. The rule requiring one to marry outside the group is called the principle of:
    a. Endogamy
    b. Exogamy
    c. Bigamy

5. Approximately how many ethnic groups are there in the United States?
    a. 5
    b. 15
    c. 150

6. Mrs. Friendly thinks of and treats her best friend Mrs. Keck as family. As such, Mrs. Keck is considered:
    a. Family of procreation
    b. Family of orientation
    c. Fictive Kin

7. Peter attends his annual family reunion and knows that the attractive women that he meets there are not to be viewed as potential mates because they are his relatives. This rule, which prohibits sexual relations among relatives, is known as the:
    a. Exclusive Family Clause
    b. Incest taboo
    c. Fictive kin

8. Jerome and Dee Dee marry and move in with Jerome's parents. This illustrates which type of marriage?
    a. Patrilocal
    b. Matrilocal
    c. Neolocal

9. Victor lives in New York City and is married to Nikki. Victor does not divorce Nikki before he marries Faith. This illegal practice of having two wives is called?
    a. Monogamy
    b. Bigamy
    c. Exogamy

10. Brad and Angelina would prefer that their white, upper-class, American child marry someone who is white, upper class, and American. The rule requiring one to stay within a group is known as the principle of:
   a. Endogamy
   b. Exogamy
   c. Bigamy

11. Louise and George have one son, Lionel, who is 23 years old. Recently, Lionel moved out, leaving Louise and George alone. This departure of grown children from the household results in the:
   a. Boomerang generation
   b. Empty nest syndrome
   c. Early widowhood

12. In many Muslim countries, the male is allowed to have up to four wives. This practice of a man having many wives at once is known as:
   a. Polygyny
   b. Polyandry
   c. Serial monogamy

13. The average age of the American population is:
   a. Declining
   b. Increasing
   c. Staying the same

14. Juan and Maria Ortega are a married couple with one child. The Ortegas live with Maria's mother and father. Which type of family is illustrated?
   a. Extended
   b. Nuclear
   c. Fictive

15. Maresha and Brian have been living together and engaging in a sexual relationship for the past 15 years. Although they have never had a wedding ceremony, they have a:
   a. Ceremonial marriage
   b. Common-law marriage
   c. Cohabitation marriage

16. Joey and Chandler are best friends & roommates. This illustrates a:
   a. Non-family household
   b. Empty nest family
   c. Nuclear family

17. Homer and Marge are a married couple with three biological children. This family is a/an:
    a. Extended family
    b. Nuclear family
    c. Empty nest family

18. Kelly was raised by her parents, Al and Peggy. Al and Peggy make up Kelly's:
    a. Family of orientation
    b. Family of procreation
    c. Fictive kin

19. Eric and Stephanie work hard at their jobs to provide food, clothing and shelter for their children. This illustrates which function of family?
    a. Emotional support
    b. Socialization
    c. Economic security

20. When Ray remembers his childhood he realizes that no one ever hugged him, kissed him, or told him that he was loved. His family failed to accomplish which function?
    a. Socialization
    b. Emotional support
    c. Regulation of sexual behavior

21. Most of the people who attend that very prestigious University are similar in their families' level of wealth, education, power and prestige. As such, they are in the same:
    a. Social Class
    b. Ethnic Group
    c. Racial Group

22. It has been suggested that there are more single people today because the women's rights movement transformed gender roles. This is an example of a ____ explanation.
    a. Macro-level
    b. Micro-level
    c. Societal-level

23. The grandparents of the present day tend to be _____ grandparents of previous years.
   a. Younger than
   b. Older than
   c. The same age as

24. Jennifer and Ben had a baby and named her Violet. Violet is a part of Jen and Ben's:
   a. Family of orientation
   b. Family of procreation
   c. Extended Family

25. Michelle and James marry and move in with Michelle's parents. This illustrates which type of marriage?
   a. Patrilocal
   b. Matrilocal
   c. Neolocal

APPLICATIONS/EXERCISES

1. There are three broad perspectives on the changing family. Which perspective is portrayed on your favorite family television shows? What makes you say this?

2. According to the text, the family fulfills several important functions. Think about your own family. How does it work to fulfill the five functions of family? Give specific examples.

3. Consider the three residential patterns in family. Which one is most suitable for you and your family? Why?

CHAPTER 1 KEY TERMS CROSSWORD PUZZLE

Across
5. Household with non-relatives
7. One person married to one other
10. Network of relatives
11. Forbids sex within family
14. Group offering close contact
15. Focused on large-scale
17. Marry outside the group
18. Family with husband, wife & kids
19. Illegally marry a 2nd spouse
20. Focused on individuals
24. Couple gets a new residence
25. One person has 2+ spouses
26. Disruptive
27. Family one is born into
28. When he has many wives

29. Obligations & expectations
Down
1. Group that is short-term
2. Here, it is okay to mate
3. Family formed by having children
4. Marriage through cohabitation
6. Promotes social solidarity
8. People that are like family
9. Teaching children to do right
12. Multi-generational family
13. Rules for behavior
14. When she has many husbands
16. Couple lives with his family
21. Marry within the group
22. Category having similar rank
23. Couple lives with her family

POST-TEST

1. Theresa and Bob have been married eight years. Their marriage illustrates the three main characteristics of marriage. As such, there is shared economic responsibility, _____ and bearing/raising children.
   a. Living together
   b. Socialization
   c. Monogamous sexual union

2. Ibrahima has three wives living with him now and he hopes to marry another within the next year. This practice of having many wives at the same time is called:
   a. Serial monogamy
   b. Monogamy
   c. Polygyny

3. Jequisha is a middle class African-American woman and her family expects that she will marry a middle class, African-American man. This rule, requiring one to marry within a certain group, is known as the principle of _____.
   a. Incest
   b. Endogamy
   c. Exogamy

4. Fran and Gerald date for six months and decide it is time to meet one another's family. At the meeting of the families, Fran and Gerald find out that they are related. They stop seeing each other immediately. This illustrates which cultural norm that forbids sexual relations between close relatives?
   a. Monogamy rule
   b. Endogamy rule
   c. Incest taboo

5. Rebecca was adopted by the Pratt family and they raised her for 17 years. As such, the Pratt family makes up Rebecca's:
   a. Family of orientation
   b. Family of procreation
   c. Nuclear family

6. Martha and George believe that it is their responsibility to provide guidelines for their child to select a spouse. This refers to which function of family?
   a. Procreation
   b. Regulation of sexual behavior
   c. Economic cooperation

9

7. Olga married Rex and his brother. As such, Olga has 2 husbands. This form of marriage in which a wife has more than one husband is called:
   a. Serial monogamy
   b. Polyandry
   c. Polygyny

8. Which of the following is true in the United States?
   a. The percentage of married couple households is increasing
   b. The percentage of married couple households is decreasing
   c. The percentage of married couple household is staying the same

9. Nancy and Ronald have been married for 26 years. They had 3 children and all of their children have moved out of the house. Now, Nancy and Ronald are experiencing the:
   a. Empty nest syndrome
   b. Sandwich generation
   c. Non-family household

10. Ashley & Cole were both born and raised in San Francisco. After marrying, the couple moved away from both of their families to start a new life in Chicago. This illustrates which residential pattern?
    a. Patrilocal
    b. Neolocal
    c. Matrilocal

11. Cynthia does not want to have children. She does not even like children. Yet, Cynthia's mother assures her that all women are mothers by nature. This idea supports the myth of:
    a. The self sufficient family
    b. Naturalism
    c. The family as a loving refuge

12. The senior citizens who meet for the weekly lunch at the City Park often complain that the young people of today adhere to a "me-first" selfishness and lack family commitment. These senior citizens suggest that the family is:
    a. Deteriorating
    b. Changing, not deteriorating
    c. Stronger than ever

13. Which of the following demographic trends is true?
    a. Fertility rates have increased.
    b. The number of ethnic minorities has increased.
    c. The average age of the population has decreased.

14. The Camden family is made up of a mother, father, and children. This is an example of a/an _____ family.
    a. Extended
    b. Nuclear
    c. Ceremonial

15. Families are characterized by close, long lasting, intimate, face-to-face contact. As such, families are a:
    a. Primary group
    b. Secondary group
    c. Social Class

16. More young women are using birth control today than ever before. Some explain that this is because of technological changes. Which type of explanation is this?
    a. Micro-level
    b. Macro-level
    c. Individual

17. Ralph is in the 1st grade. He does not respect authority or personal property. Ralph's teacher believes that he lacks the skills needed to function effectively. She meets with Ralph's parents to discuss which family function?
    a. Procreation
    b. Socialization
    c. Emotional support

18. A cross-cultural approach is best for the study of marriage & family because:
    a. The world is a global community.
    b. U.S. businesses desire employees with knowledge of other cultures.
    c. Both a & b

19. Growing up, Teresa always recognized her mother's best friend Angela as family. Even though Angela is not a blood relative, Teresa calls her "Aunt Angela" and includes her in all family gatherings. Angela is considered:
    a. Kinship system
    b. Fictive kin
    c. Non-household family

20. Dong married Okim and she died. Ten years later Dong takes his second wife, Thuy. This practice of having two spouses at different times is called:
   a. Serial monogamy
   b. Polygamy
   c. Monogamy

21. Martin and Coretta had three children. By having these children Martin and Coretta fulfilled which function of family?
   a. Socialization
   b. Emotional support
   c. Procreation

22. Vianica is from Venezuela. Carlos is from Columbia. The two meet while in school in the U.S. They marry and live in Columbia near Carlos's family. This illustrates which residential pattern?
   a. Patrilocal
   b. Matrilocal
   c. Neolocal

23. Lucy and Ricky adopt a child and raise him as their own. The family which includes mother, father, and adopted child is a _____ family.
   a. Extended
   b. Nuclear
   c. Fictive

24. Lois is a single-parent, drug addict. Because of her addiction, Lois has not paid the rent, bought any food, or provided any clothes for her children. Lois is failing to provide for the physical needs of her family. As such, Lois has failed to carry out which function of family?
   a. Economic security
   b. Emotional support
   c. Socialization

25. Which of the following is true?
   a. Women are having fewer children today than in previous years
   b. Women are having more children today than in previous years
   c. Women are having the same number of children today as in previous years

SELF-ASSESSMENT:
HOW ENDOGAMOUS IS YOUR FAMILY?

Directions: Put a check in the box to reflect whether you agree or disagree with the following statements.

	Agree	Disagree
My family would prefer that I marry someone who shares my nationality.		
Most marriages in my family are between members of the same racial group.		
My family expects me to marry one of my relatives.		
The people in my family tend to marry members of the same religious group.		
My family would prefer that I marry within my social class.		
Most marriages in my family are between members of the same educational background.		
My family expects me to select a mate from my racial group.		
The people in my family tend to marry members of the same social class.		
My family would not like it if I married a person who does not share my religious beliefs.		
Most marriages in my family are between members of the same age group.		
My family would prefer that I marry a person who shares my educational background.		
Most marriages in my family are between relatives.		
My family would not like it if I married someone twice my age.		
Most marriages in my family are between members of the same nationality.		

Key: Give yourself 1 point for every statement that you checked as 'Agree.' A score of 14 represents the most endogamous family. A score of 0 represents a family that is not endogamous.

ANSWERS

PRE-TEST

Answers	Page Numbers
1. A	5
2. B	11
3. B	22
4. B	9
5. C	22
6. C	6
7. B	8
8. A	12
9. B	5
10. A	9
11. B	20
12. A	11
13. B	20
14. A	11
15. B	5
16. A	20
17. B	7
18. A	11
19. C	9
20. B	10
21. A	10
22. B	24
23. A	20
24. B	11
25. B	12

KEY TERMS CROSSWORD PUZZLE

Across	Page Numbers
5. Non-family	20
7. Monogamy	11
10. Kinship	11
11. Incest taboo	8
14. Primary	10
15. Macro-level	23
17. Exogamy	9
18. Nuclear	7
19. Bigamy	5
20. Micro-level	23
24. Neolocal	12
25. Polygamy	11
26. Dysfunctional	13
27. Orientation	11
28. Polygyny	11
29. Roles	9

Down

1. Secondary	10

2.	Marriage	4
3.	Procreation	11
4.	Common-law	5
6.	Functional	14
8.	Fictive Kin	6
9.	Socialization	9
12.	Extended	11
13.	Norms	4
14.	Polygyny	11
16.	Patrilocal	12
21.	Endogamy	9
22.	Social Class	10
23.	Matrilocal	12

POST-TEST

Answers	Page Numbers
1. C	4
2. C	11
3. B	9
4. C	9
5. A	11
6. B	8
7. B	11
8. B	20
9. A	20
10. B	12
11. B	14
12. A	17
13. B	22
14. B	7
15. A	10
16. B	24
17. B	9
18. C	27
19. B	6
20. A	11
21. C	9
22. C	12
23. B	7
24. A	9
25. A	20

2

STUDYING MARRIAGE AND THE FAMILY

CHAPTER OBJECTIVES

Upon reading Chapter Two, students should be able to:

1. Explain why theories and research are important in everyday life.

2. Compare and contrast the eight theories of marriage and family.

3. Discuss the relationship between research and social issues.

4. Describe the six methods of data collection in family research and discuss the strengths and weaknesses of each.

5. Recognize the ethical and political issues associated with social science research and explain the guidelines for professional conduct.

CHAPTER OVERVIEW

Studying research methods and theory is important because it provides us with accurate information, a better understanding of our own families, and the tools needed to make more informed decisions. A **theory** is a set of statements that explain why a phenomenon occurs. The first theory is the **ecological perspective,** which studies the relationship between individuals and their social environment. According to this theory, there are four interlocking systems that mold a child's developmental growth: microsystem, mesosystem, exosystem and macrosystem. The **structural-functionalist approach** is the second theory. It examines the relationship between the family and larger society, as well as how the different parts of a family's structure work together to fulfill the **functions**, or tasks necessary for the family's survival. Anything that interferes with the fulfillment of social functions is seen as **dysfunctional**. Functions can be **manifest** (recognized and intended) or **latent** (unrecognized and unintended). In the traditional family, adult family tasks are best accomplished when the husband plays the **instrumental role** (providing food and shelter) and the wife plays the **expressive role** (homemaking and emotional support).

Conflict theory examines the ways in which groups disagree, struggle over power, and compete for scarce resources. Society is full of inequality and there is a continuous struggle between the *"haves"* and the *"have-nots."* **Feminist theories** are the offspring of conflict theory, and they examine how gender roles (expectations about how men and women should behave) shape relations between women and men. A feminist is any person who believes that both sexes should have equal rights. Three categories of feminism are: *liberal feminism* (create equal opportunities for women), *radical feminism* (male domination is a major cause of women's inequality), and *global feminism* (women in the developing world are exploited). Most feminist research uses **qualitative research** (based on observations and interviews), rather than **quantitative research** (based on an assignment of numbers to observations by counting and measuring).

Symbolic interaction theory examines how our ideas, beliefs, and attitudes shape our daily lives. According to this theory, effective interaction is based on *shared meanings* (agreed upon definitions) that we learn from our *significant others* (people in primary groups who play an important role in our socialization). Symbolic interaction theory is the first *micro-level theory*, as it looks at the everyday behaviors of individuals. Another micro-level theory is social exchange. **Social exchange theory**, the second micro-theory, posits that people make decisions and choices based on perceived costs and rewards in an attempt to maximize rewards and reduce costs. Social exchange theorists argue that most people will continue in a relationship only as long as it is more rewarding than costly. **Family life course development theory** examines the changes that families experience over the lifespan. The family life cycle consists of transitions that a family makes as it moves through stages and events. In the classic model, the family life cycle begins with marriage and ends with the death of one or both partners. The **family systems theory**, the final micro-level perspective, views the family as a functioning unit that solves problems, makes decisions, and achieves collective goals. This theory focuses on the rules that hold families together.

Social scientists use six major research methods to answer questions about the family. **Surveys** are used to systematically collect data from respondents through interviews or questionnaires. Researchers typically draw a **sample**, a group of people that represent the population under study. **Clinical research** examines individuals or small groups who seek help from mental health professionals and other scientists. Clinical research relies on the *case study method*, which provides detailed information about family life. Clinical practitioners also use interviews, direct observation, and record analysis. In **field research**, data is collected by systematically observing people in their natural surroundings. Field research includes two types of observation: participant and nonparticipant. In *participant observation*, researchers interact naturally with the people they are studying but do not reveal their identities as researchers. In *nonparticipant* observation, researchers study phenomena without being a part of the situation. In **secondary analysis**, researchers use data collected by someone else. Because secondary data are often *longitudinal* (information collected at two or more points in time) rather than *cross-sectional* (information collected at one point in time), it allows researchers to examine trends over time. **Experiments** investigate cause and effect relationships under strictly controlled conditions. A researcher tests a prediction or hypothesis that one variable causes another. **Evaluation research** measures the efficiency and effectiveness of social programs in both the public and private sectors. Such research is applied, providing program administrators with information to improve or initiate services.

The legitimacy of social science research becomes suspect to political and religious groups when the focus is on sensitive social, moral, and political issues. The federal government and many professional organizations have codes of ethics to protect research participants.

PRE-TEST

1. Anisa is studying behavioral differences between males and females at college football games. Anisa attends the local football game dressed in the school colors. She makes observations without revealing herself as a researcher. This is an example of:
   a. Participants observation
   b. Non-participant observation
   c. Secondary analysis

2. Jason enjoys playing football. Through his interactions with his older brother Steven, Jason learned that football was a good way to exercise, spend time with friends, and show off his athletic skills. Because of this influence on his younger brother, symbolic interaction theorists would refer to Steven as a:
   a. Significant other
   b. Instrumental role
   c. Expressive role

3. Riham wants to know the percentage of students at her college that come from step-families. Riham selects a group of 1,000 students to represent the larger population. This group of 1,000 is called a:
   a. Cross-section
   b. Sample
   c. Sub-population

4. To Snoop, sex outside of marriage means a good time. To Denzel, sex outside of marriage means sin and regret. Which theory best explains how the two men develop such different meanings for the same thing?
   a. Conflict
   b. Symbolic interaction
   c. Family Systems

5. Making friends and meeting potential mates are examples of the _____ function of education.
   a. Instrumental
   b. Manifest
   c. Latent

6. Naomi wants to know if people are more supportive of sexual scenes being shown on prime time drama television shows or on day time soap opera television shows. Her research involves telephone interviews. This study employs which research method?
   a. Survey
   b. Experiment
   c. Secondary analysis

7. Bob believes that men and women should have equal political, social, and economic rights. Which type of feminist is Bob?
   a. Liberal
   b. Global
   c. Radical

8. Which theorists would be most interested in explaining how the Democrats and Republicans in American government disagree, struggle over power, and compete for scarce resources?
   a. Symbolic interaction theorists
   b. Social exchange theorists
   c. Conflict theorists

9. A common misconception about feminists is that:
   a.   Feminists are always women
   b.   Feminists hate men
   c.   Both a & b

10. Keron wants to gain a greater understanding of the polygamous men in Senegal, so he goes to live among them to observe them as an outsider. This is an example of which type of field research?
   a. Participant observation
   b. Non-participant observation
   c. Clinical observation

11. Most of the research that was recently presented at the national Marriage & Family Conference involved questionnaires that asked yes/no questions and then assigned a 1 for questions answered yes and a 0 for questions answered no. This type of research is called:
   a. Quantitative
   b. Qualitative
   c. Secondary

12. To protect research participants, many professional organizations have:
   a. Hired administrators to approve and review all research projects
   b. Imposed fines for researchers who do not follow directions
   c. Developed ethics codes

13. The tasks needed for a family to survive include procreation, economic security, and emotional support. These are examples of family _____.
   a. Functions
   b. Ethics
   c. Dysfunctions

14. The fundamental premise of _____ theory is that any social interaction between two people is based on the efforts of each person to maximize rewards and minimize costs
   a. Conflict
   b. Social exchange
   c. Symbolic interaction

15. In the Keane family, the wife is the breadwinner and the husband is the homemaker. The wife, Mrs. Keane, is fulfilling the:
   a. Instrumental role
   b. Expressive role
   c. Both a & b

16. Which theory was born out of conflict theory?
   a. Social exchange
   b. Family systems
   c. Feminist

17. Roger is 35 years old and still lives with his parents, the Finklesteins. The Finklesteins believe that in order to get Roger to leave, they should make his stay in their home less comfortable. Which theory supports this idea that a person will end a relationship when the costs outweigh the benefits?
    a. Family system
    b. Family life cycle development
    c. Social exchange

18. Recent research suggests that welfare to work programs, which provide the poor with temporary jobs, do more economic harm than good for the families in the program. The type of research that produced such findings probably involves:
    a. Experiment
    b. Secondary analysis
    c. Evaluation

19. Vera received a grant to study the Christmas-Eve shopping patterns of local parents. Vera and her team surveyed a random sample of shoppers. This research, which was collected only at one point in time, is:
    a. Cross-sectional
    b. Longitudinal
    c. Both a & b

20. It is important for students to study research methods and theory because it helps:
    a. In informed decision making
    b. Students understand their own families
    c. Both a & b

21. By having a child, Makiyo and Sachi ensure that their family will live on into the future. This illustrates the _____ function of procreation.
    a. Latent
    b. Manifest
    c. Expressive

22. To many people, the American flag is a symbol of freedom and democracy. According to the symbolic interaction perspective, this agreed upon definition is a:
    a. Significant other
    b. Symbol
    c. Shared meaning

23. Which theory is least likely to examine people who are single?
    a. Symbolic interaction
    b. Social exchange
    c. Family life course development

24. Scott wants to know if regular exercise causes enhanced sexual performance. Which method of research would be best for this study of cause and effect?
    a. Secondary analysis
    b. Experiment
    c. Evaluation

25. After traveling to West Africa on a study abroad excursion, Miranda decided to organize a student group to fight the exploitation of women in the developing world. As such, Miranda is which type of feminist?
    a. Liberal
    b. Global
    c. Radical

APPLICATIONS/EXERCISES

1. The structural-functional perspective suggests that families are most effective when the husband performs the instrumental role and the wife performs the expressive role. How does this support or refute your ideas about family roles? How do you envision your own family?

2. Feminists believe that both sexes should have equal rights. Ask 5 of your friends/family members if they are feminists. After they answer, give them the definition from the text. Does this definition impact their answers?

CHAPTER 2 KEY TERMS CROSSWORD PUZZLE

Across

3. Research that assigns numbers
4. Family ____ Cycle
5. Family Life ____ Development
7. Explains why
9. Observing people in natural setting
10. Considers the environment
12. Gives cause & effect
14. Theory studying haves & have nots
15. Analysis which borrows data
17. Represents the population
18. Unrecognized

19. Wants equality among the sexes
20. Interviews & Questionnaires
21. Research from respondents' POV

Down

1. Homemaker role
2. Suggests rules hold families together
6. Theory of add pros, subtract cons
8. Research assessing efficiency
11. How men and women should behave
13. Breadwinner role
16. Intended

POST-TEST

1. Researchers at the local University are trying to explain the recent increase in the number of teen-pregnancies. The researchers are developing a:
   a. Theory
   b. Family life cycle
   c. Manifest function

2. Which theorists are most likely to focus on why men get a higher starting salary than women in the same position, even when they have the same levels of education and experience?
   a. Feminist
   b. Social exchange
   c. Symbolic interaction

3. Ray works hard at his job so that he can provide food and shelter for his family. According to the structural-functionalist perspective, Ray is fulfilling the _____ role.
   a. Manifest
   b. Expressive
   c. Instrumental

4. Debra is a homemaker. She cooks, cleans, and provides emotional support for her family. According to the structural-functionalist perspective, Debra is fulfilling the _____ role.
   a. Manifest
   b. Expressive
   c. Instrumental

5. Which theory focuses on the rules that hold families together?
   a. Family systems
   b. Family life course development
   c. Symbolic interaction

6. Which theory focuses on the various stages through which families transition?
   a. Family life course development
   b. Family systems
   c. Symbolic interaction

7. Interviews and questionnaires are used in which method of research?
   a. Experiments
   b. Observation
   c. Surveys

8. Hilda is conducting a research project for her class and needs to uncover a cause-effect relationship between relationship dynamics and moods. Which method of social research should Hilda use?
   a. Experiments
   b. Observation
   c. Surveys

9. Brad uses data already collected by the local Health Department to determine the characteristics of people that are most likely to be tested for HIV. Brad has engaged in which mode of research?
   a. Secondary analysis
   b. Experiments
   c. Clinical Research

10. Dr. Barber is a researcher who studies how children's social environment influences development. Dr. Barber subscribes to _____ theory.
    a. Family systems
    b. Social exchange
    c. Ecological

11. Keoko is investigating how mother-daughter relationships change over time. As such, she collects information from the families once a year over the course of 6 years. This type is study in which data is collected on more than one occasion is called:
    a. Longitudinal
    b. Sample
    c. Cross-sectional

12. When families divorce, the functions of family are disrupted. As such, the structural functional perspective views divorce as:
    a. Functional
    b. Dysfunctional
    c. Instrumental

13. Which theory suggests that society is full of inequality and struggle?
    a. Social exchange
    b. Conflict
    c. Structural Functional

14. The local university recently hired a consultant to determine if efforts to recruit more minority students have been effective. Which type of research is this?
    a. Secondary Analysis
    b. Survey
    c. Evaluation

15. Participant observation and non-participant observation are forms of which type of research?
    a. Clinical
    b. Survey
    c. Field

16. The case study method is employed in which type of research studies?
    a. Clinical
    b. Survey
    c. Evaluation

17. Sharonda is studying the competition for scarce resources between blacks and whites in America. Which theoretical perspective is Sharonda most likely to use?
    a. Feminist
    b. Social exchange
    c. Conflict

18. Symbolic interaction, social exchange, family life course development, and family systems theories are all _____ theories.
    a. Macro-level
    b. Micro-level
    c. Conflict

19. Reba feels like she gives and gives and gives but that her husband does not give back. Which theory suggests that Reba's marriage will end if her benefits do not increase?
    a. Social exchange
    b. Family systems
    c. Family life course development

20. Dr. Jackson is a psychologist. The patients who visit his office for mental health treatment are a part of his research. The patients provide Dr. Jackson with detailed information about their family life. This illustrates which type of research?
    a. Experiment
    b. Clinical
    c. Secondary analysis

21. Brenda argues that male domination is responsible for inequality between men and women. Brenda is which type of feminist?
    a. Liberal
    b. Global
    c. Radical

22. A wedding is a social gathering where two people make a public commitment. Often, the couple receives wedding gifts to help them set up a household. The gifts are a/an _____ function of weddings.
   a. Latent
   b. Manifest
   c. Instrumental

23. In Abdul's Marriage & Family class, the students have to observe how couples interact in public places. This observational research is:
   a. Quantitative
   b. Qualitative
   c. Both a & b

24. Which theory suggests that there are four interlocking systems that impact a child's development?
   a. Family systems
   b. Social exchange
   c. Ecological

25. Which theory suggests that the family life cycle begins with marriage and ends with the death of one or both partners?
   a. Family system
   b. Family life course development
   c. Feminist

SELF-ASSESSMENT:
ARE YOU A FEMINIST?

Directions: Put a check in the box to reflect whether you agree or disagree with the following statements.

	Agree	Disagree
Men are more effective in political office than women.		
Husbands should make more money than their wives.		
Women should do the cooking and cleaning in a family.		
Women should not serve in the military.		
Fathers do not have the capacity to be as nurturing as mothers.		
A woman should submit to her husband.		
A man's major responsibility to his family is providing.		
Daughters need more help than sons.		
Women should be excluded from military drafts.		
I have more respect for male police officers than female police officers.		
Women are too emotional.		
I would prefer to have a male boss over a female boss.		
Since men are breadwinners, they should get paid more than women.		
Children should spend more time with their mothers than their fathers.		
In a dual earner family, when the children are sick, the mother should take off from work to take care of them.		
A woman's major responsibility to her family is homemaking.		
A man should be the head of the household.		
Men are more ambitious than women.		
Most women attend college to find a husband.		
Sons should be able to stay out later than daughters.		

Key: Give yourself 1 point for every statement that you checked as 'Disagree.' A score of 0 represents the most feminist viewpoints. A score of 20 represents a person who opposes sexual equality. A score of 10 represents mixed ambivalence.

ANSWERS

PRE-TEST

Answers	Page Numbers
1. A	48
2. A	39
3. B	44
4. B	39
5. C	37
6. A	44
7. A	38
8. C	37
9. C	38
10. B	48
11. A	38
12. C	52
13. A	37
14. B	40
15. B	37
16. C	38
17. B	40
18. C	50
19. A	38
20. C	32
21. B	37
22. C	39
23. C	40
24. B	49
25. B	38

KEY TERMS CROSSWORD PUZZLE

Across	Page Numbers
3. Quantitative	38
4. Life	41
5. Course	40
7. Theory	34
9. Field Research	48
10. Ecological	35
12. Experiment	49
14. Conflict	37
15. Secondary	48
17. Sample	44
18. Latent	37
19. Feminist	38
20. Survey	44
21. Qualitative	38

Down

1. Expressive	37

POST-TEST

Answers	**Page Numbers**
1. A	34
2. A	38
3. C	37
4. B	37
5. A	42
6. A	40
7. C	44
8. A	49
9. A	48
10. C	35
11. A	49
12. B	37
13. B	37
14. C	50
15. C	47
16. A	47
17. C	37
18. B	39
19. A	40
20. B	47
21. C	38
22. A	37
23. B	38
24. C	35
25. A	41

THE FAMILY IN HISTORICAL PERSPECTIVE

3

CHAPTER OBJECTIVES

Upon reading Chapter Three, students should be able to:

1. Discuss the characteristics of Puritan families in colonial times.

2. Discuss the central characteristics of Native American families in colonial times and describe the impact of European culture on Native-American family structure.

3. Discuss the central characteristics of African-American families during colonial times and explain popular misconceptions about the effects of slavery.

4. Discuss the central characteristics of Mexican American families during colonial times and describe their economic exploitation by Europeans.

5. Explain how European immigration impacted family life.

6. Explain how the Industrial Revolution impacted family life.

7. Describe the companionate family.

8. Explain how World War II impacted family life.

9. Describe the emergence of the modern family.

10. Identify the problems that families faced in the "Nifty Fifties."

CHAPTER OVERVIEW

In colonial times, the nuclear family was the most prevalent family form. The family was a self-sufficient unit that acted as a business, a school, a vocational institute, a church, a house of correction, and a welfare institute. Predominant characteristics of the colonial family include the prevalence of premarital and extramarital sex, the subordination of women, a high death rate for children, an expectation that children would be well-behaved, and the pervasiveness of child labor. The Puritans tried to prevent premarital sex by **bundling**, which is when a fully dressed young man and woman spent the night in bed together, separated by a wooden board. Three distinct social class divisions were evident: *merchant class* (upper), *artisan class* (middle), and *laboring class* (working).

Many American Indians were **matrilineal** (tracing descent through mother's line), while others were **patrilineal** (tracing descent through the father's line). Indian women were often better off than white women, serving as chiefs, doctors, politicians and warriors. Because of high infant and child death rates, most Indian families were small. Childhood was a happy time and grandparents were active in the lives of grandchildren. Europeans destroyed much of Indian culture through military slaughter, enslavement, forced labor, land confiscation, coerced mass migration, and involuntary religious conversions.

It was commonly believed that slavery destroyed the African-American family, but recent research suggests that the family structure was resilient. Yet, it was difficult for slaves to marry and often the marriages did not last long. Male slaves often served as the surrogate father to many children. Female slaves worked a *'double day,'* a full day of domestic chores plus a full day of work outside the home. Slave children as young as 2 years old worked. After emancipation, many families were reunited and many marriages were formalized.

Mexican-American families were dispossessed of their lands and colonized by European-American settlers. Despite this economic exploitation, Mexican families were characterized by **familism**, where family relationships took precedence over individual well being. A key factor in conserving the Mexican culture was **compadrazgo**, in which parents, children, and godparents established and maintained close relationships. *Compadres* or co-parents were godparents who enlarged family ties and provided discipline and support. Females, who were primarily homemakers and mothers, were the guardians of family tradition. Males, who served as the head of the family had all authority. Masculinity was expressed in the concept of **machismo**, which stresses male attributes like dominance, assertiveness, pride, and sexual prowess.

Industrialization brought about mechanization which shifted home manufacturing to large-scale factory production. As the economic structure changed, family life was altered: husbands went out to work as *breadwinners*; wives stayed home as *housewives*; couples were freer to choose mates; ties with the community weakened; spouses turned to each other for affection; *true womanhood* redefined the role of wife as caregiver; fathers lost some control over children; and children were viewed as more than 'miniature adults'.

Between 1830 and 1932, two massive waves of immigrants arrived in the U.S. from Europe. Immigration played a key role in the industrial transformation by providing a pool of cheap labor. Many immigrants were subjected to poverty, poor housing, chronic health problems, family conflict, prejudice, and discrimination.

At the turn of the twentieth century, married couples began to stress the importance of sexual attraction and compatibility in their relationships, which gave rise to the *companionate family.* Also, children and parents expressed affection more openly, and adolescents enjoyed greater freedom.

The Great Depression had devastating effects on working-class families, who experienced widespread unemployment and confinement to low-paying jobs. African-Americans suffered even more as unemployment was higher among blacks. In many families, unemployment impacted gender roles because the authority of the husband/father was tied to his role as provider. In 1932, a federal executive order decreed that only one spouse could work for the federal government, pressuring women to quit their jobs. When women did work, they were paid less than men.

When the U.S. entered WWII in 1941, family life changed. Because many able-bodied men had been drafted, many women found well-paying jobs and were praised for working outside the home. At the end of the war, divorce rates reached a new high as some wives who had worked during the war and enjoyed economic independence ended unhappy marriages. Still other families were disrupted by alcoholism (the leading cause for divorce), incapacitation, and incompatibility. When returning veterans needed jobs and women were no longer needed in the workplace, ideas about family roles changed. The "Golden Fifties" saw the roles of women transform to pleasing their husbands and being full-time housewives. Having children and living in the suburbs was considered desirable. A generation of **baby boomers**, people born between 1946 and 1964, entered the world. Yet, families experienced many problems: consumerism was limited to the middle and upper class; minorities faced severe discrimination; domestic violence and child abuse were widespread; young people were forced into shotgun marriages; childcare services were almost nonexistent for working mothers; and alcohol and drug use soared. Over the last 30 years, family structure, gender, and economic concerns have changed.

PRE-TEST
1. The year is 1837 and Victoria is learning the graces of true womanhood. She is learning that women are 'good' if they are:
   a. Submissive
   b. Sexy
   c. Eager

2. The year is 1910 and Tom & Helen Willis both believe that sexual attraction and compatibility are important in their marriage. The two share affection with one another as well as their daughter, Jenny. This illustrates:
   a. The companionate family
   b. Familism
   c. Bundling

3. The Alvarez family maintains close contact with their children's godparents. This illustrates:
   a. Familism
   b. Compadrazgo
   c. Machismo

4. Which class was most impacted by the Great Depression?
   a. Working class
   b. Middle class
   c. Upper class

5. World War II has just ended and Myrtle wants to divorce her husband of 12 years. A common explanation for Myrtle's desire is based on:
   a. Extramarital affairs
   b. Economic independence
   c. The sexual revolution

6. Joe is a blacksmith in 1860. Because he is in a highly skilled occupation, Joe belongs to which social class?
   a. Merchant
   b. Artisan
   c. Laboring

7. William traveled fourteen miles in the snow to visit his girlfriend Mary in 1757. Because of the long walk home, Mary's parents allowed William to stay the night. William and Mary slept in the bed together but were separated by a wooden board. This is called:
   a. Cuddling
   b. Purifying

    c. Bundling

8. The year is 1932 and the federal government has just decreed that:
    a. Blacks are not allowed to work for the federal government
    b. Schools will be closed so that children can look for work
    c. Only one spouse can work for the federal government

9. Elizabeth is about to get married in colonial America. Her mother is informing her of a wife's chief duty. Her mother tells her, "A wife's chief duty is to _____."
    a. Have children
    b. Be frugal
    c. Obey her husband

10. Which group did not come to North America voluntarily?
    a. African Americans
    b. American Indians
    c. Mexican Americans

11. When Amelia asks her husband Carlos to help her hang the laundry out to dry, Carlos tells her that he is a man, and as a man, it is not fitting for him to do women's work. This illustrates:
    a. Familism
    b. Compadrazgo
    c. Machismo

12. Adsila and Kotori are a Native American married couple. Their children trace their family heritage through their mother's family line. This illustrates a _____ family.
    a. Patrilineal
    b. Matrilineal
    c. Bi-lineal

13. In Mexican-American families, _____ were considered the guardians of family traditions.
    a. Women
    b. Men
    c. Children

14. Although Ernesto does not make a whole lot of money, he sends more than ½ of his pay check to his family. In Ernesto's mind, family relationships take precedence over individual well-being. This illustrates:
    a. Compadrazgo
    b. Machismo
    c. Familism

15. During the Great Depression, Arthur lost the position of authority in his house. This is explained by the fact that:
    a. A man's authority was tied to his role as provider
    b. Arthur's children became more independent and rebellious
    c. Both a & b

16. Wanda is the married mother of 3 sons. Wanda works at the local factory and she is praised by government, the media, and her family for working. In which period was this typical?
    a. The Great Depression
    b. During World War II
    c. The Nifty 1950's

17. The Smiths make and sell soap so that they can trade it for eggs and candles. This depicts the family as a:
    a. Vocational institute
    b. Business
    c. Welfare institution

18. Thomas Price is a student at the local high school. With his teacher's help, Thomas has traced his family back 200 years to his great-great uncle Silas. When Thomas's childhood is compared to Silas's, who was probably expected to be better-behaved?
    a. Thomas
    b. Silas
    c. No-difference

19. The Walkers lost their family business when commercial factories replaced them. Because of _____, home manufacturing shifted to large scale factory production.
    a. The Industrial Revolution
    b. World War II
    c. European immigration

20. In colonial America, which women were most likely to serve as physicians and politicians?
    a. Native Americans
    b. Mexican Americans
    c. European Americans

21. The year is 1860. Wayne is a shipping entrepreneur. He belongs to which class?
    a. Merchant
    b. Artisan
    c. Laboring

22. Polly works a double day in colonial America. After a full day of domestic chores, she has a full day of work outside the home. Polly is most likely?
    a. Native-American
    b. Mexican American
    c. African-American

23. The year is 1830. Otis is orphaned after his parents die in a fire. Otis moves in with his aunt and uncle. This depicts the family as a:
    a. Vocational institute
    b. House of correction
    c. Welfare institution

24. In 1890, the Antonelli family immigrated to America from Italy. Which of the following characterizes what they probably faced?
    a. Prejudice and discrimination
    b. Decent housing
    c. High-paying jobs

25. Which of the following is true of colonial families?
    a. Pre-marital sex was common
    b. Pre-marital sex was uncommon
    c. Pre-marital sex was utterly foreign

APPLICATIONS/EXERCISES

1. The text notes that large-scale societal events have shaped family life since colonial times. In your life-time, one of the most severe societal events has been the 9/11 attacks. How do you think that family life in America has changed since the 9/11 attacks? Consider family roles, gender roles, ethnic groups, social class, and children.

2. During World War II, the media was used to convince women that their place was at work. After the war, media messages changed to suggest that a woman's place was at home. Think about your favorite television shows. What suggestions do the media provide for today's wife and mother? Are there mixed or consistent messages? Has the message changed since you were a child?

CHAPTER 3 KEY TERMS CROSSWORD PUZZLE

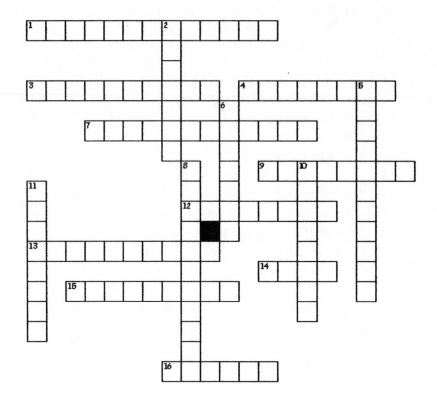

Across
1. What's good for the ladies
3. #1 cause of divorce after war
4. Masculine attributes
7. Family based on compatibility
9. Working class
12. Upper class
13. The ____ Revolution
14. War that ended in '46
15. Godparents
16. Day of work at home & outside home

Down
2. Middle class
5. Trace Mom's line
6. Born in '50
8. Close ties among Mexican Americans
10. In bed w/your love & wood
11. Family before self

POST-TEST

1. In colonial America, Little Ruth is 3 years old and she works every day, all day long. Little Ruth is probably:
   a. African-American
   b. Native-American
   c. Mexican American

2. Victor is the head of the household. He establishes this through male attributes like dominance, assertiveness, and pride. Victor is expressing:
   a. Compadrazgo
   b. Machismo
   c. Familism

3. Lawrence is a blacksmith, and he teaches his son the trade. This illustrates the family functioning as a:
   a. Vocational institute
   b. Church
   c. School

4. Arthur Fonzarelli marries Shirley Feeney, and their children trace their family descent through Arthur's line. Tracing family through the father is:
   a. Patrilineal
   b. Matrilineal
   c. Bilineal

5. Divorce rates hit an all time high after:
   a. The Great Depression
   b. The Industrial Revolution
   c. World War II

6. Rita is a working class domestic. She hears her employers talking about why a maid could never be a 'true woman'. According to them, Rita could never meet the criteria because:
   a. She works outside the home for money
   b. She engages in housework
   c. She is a virgin

7. The year is 1746. John and Abby are a New England couple and they do not want their daughter to have sex outside of marriage. John and Abby allow their daughter's boyfriend to spend the night, but they adopt which Puritan custom?
   a. Shot-gun marriage
   b. Bundling
   c. Chastity Belts

8. Angela would rather play with her friends, but each day after school she goes to help her grandmother with chores. This idea that family relationships are more important than individual well-being is called:
   a. Familism
   b. Compadrazgo
   c. Machismo

9. The year is 1946 and Betty, along with many other women, is being forced to leave her high paying job because:
   a. A law was passed banning women from working
   b. Veterans returning from the war need jobs
   c. Both a & b

10. In colonial America, it is very difficult for Amos to find a spouse. Which ethnic group members had the most difficulty finding a spouse?
    a. African-Americans
    b. Native Americans
    c. Mexican-Americans

11. Signs are posted all over town that read "A Woman's Place Is In The Workplace!" Which era is it?
    a. During the Industrial Revolution
    b. During the Great Depression
    c. During World War II

12. Ricardo and Maria asked Carlos and Juanita to be the godparents of their daughter Christina. The term for godparents used by Mexican-Americans in colonial America is:
    a. Familism
    b. Machismo
    c. Compadres

13. The major cause of the increases in divorce after World War II was:
    a. Alcoholism
    b. Extramarital affairs
    c. Economic Independence

14. Dorothy, Blanche, and Rose were all born in 1949. As such they are:
    a. Baby boomers
    b. Early bloomers
    c. Post-war babies

15. Between 35-40% of marriages among African-American slaves ended because one spouse:
    a. Died
    b. Was sold
    c. Was raped

16. The year is 2008. Beverly often wishes that she was born during colonial times. However, Beverly's teacher tells her that she would not have enjoyed it because:
    a. Most children had to work
    b. Most girls were in school all day
    c. Most children lived away from their parents

17. The year is 1842. Ana has a wonderful relationship with her grandparents. They often teach her lessons and tell her stories. The involved grandparent characterizes the _____ family.
    a. African-American
    b. Native American
    c. Mexican-American

18. The year is 1950 and Lucy and Ricky are a newly-married, working-class Hispanic couple. Which problems are they likely to face over the next decade?
    a. Discrimination
    b. Alcohol and drug use
    c. Both a & b

19. The year is 1860 and Sophia is a domestic servant. She cooks and cleans for her employers. Sophia belongs to which class.
    a. Merchant
    b. Artisan
    c. Laboring

20. During the Great Depression, 10 year old Mikey joined a group of his friends and drifted from town to town looking for work. Groups like this were called the:
    a. Little beggars
    b. Transient army
    c. Miniature adults

21. When Buck hears stories about his family history, he learns that his family survived through military slaughter, enslavement, forced labor, land confiscation, coerced mass migration, and involuntary religious conversions. Buck is a member of which ethnic group?
    a. African-Americans
    b. American Indians
    c. Mexican-Americans

22. In colonial America, Fred serves as a surrogate father to many of the children that live near him. Fred is most likely a/an:
    a. African American
    b. American Indian
    c. Mexican American

23. The year is 1951 and Sandy and Danny were just married. They are planning to move to the suburbs. They find the suburbs attractive because:
    a. The homes offer greater space and privacy
    b. It provides an escape from the dirt and noise of the city
    c. Both a & b

24. During World War II, which women made the greatest economic gains at work?
    a. Whites
    b. Blacks
    c. American Indians

25. Roger and Rachel are Puritans in colonial America. They just had a baby. The couple views their child as:
    a. Pure and innocent
    b. Sinful
    c. Both a & b

SELF-ASSESSMENT:
HOW INDEPENDENT IS YOUR FAMILY?

Directions: Put a check in the box to reflect whether you agree or disagree with the following statements.

	Agree	Disagree
The elderly members of my family who are unable to care for themselves usually live with relatives who care for them.		
My family owns and operates a business.		
I was home-schooled or educated at home by my family.		
My family worships together in the home.		
If my young relatives lost their parents in a car accident, someone in my family would probably take them in and raise them.		
My parents taught me to read.		
My family prays together in the home.		
Most of the people that baby-sit for my family are relatives.		
Most of my relatives work together in business.		
I work in my family's business.		
When members of my family are sick, we turn to one another for advice and assistance before seeking a medical professional.		
The children in my family are trained to pursue the profession of their parents.		
If a member of my family needed a loan, he/she would go to a family member before going to an outsider.		
When a family member needs someone to talk to, they usually talk to a relative.		
Most of the members of my family were birthed at home and not in a hospital.		

Key: Give yourself 1 point for every statement that you checked as 'Agree'. A score of 15 represents the most independent family, who, like colonial families, acts as a business, vocational institute, school, miniature religious entity and a welfare agency. A score of 0 represents a family who relies more on outside agencies for support.

ANSWERS

PRE-TEST

Answers	Page Numbers
1. A	71
2. A	75
3. B	70
4. A	76
5. B	77
6. B	63
7. C	60
8. C	76
9. C	61
10. A	63
11. C	70
12. B	65
13. A	70
14. C	70
15. C	76
16. B	77
17. B	60
18. B	62
19. A	71
20. A	65
21. A	62
22. C	67
23. C	60
24. A	75
25. A	61

KEY TERMS CROSSWORD PUZZLE

Across	Page Numbers
1. True Womanhood	71
3. Alcoholism	78
4. Machismo	70
7. Companionate	75
9. Laboring	63
12. Merchant	62
13. Industrial	71
14. WWII	77
15. Compadres	70
16. Double	67

Down	
2. Artisan	63
5. Matrilineal	65
6. Boomer	79
8. Compadrazgo	70
10. Bundling	60
11. Familism	70

POST-TEST

Answers	Page Numbers
1. A	67
2. B	70
3. A	60
4. A	65
5. C	77
6. A	71
7. B	60
8. A	70
9. B	78
10. A	67
11. C	77
12. C	70
13. A	78
14. A	79
15. B	67
16. A	62
17. B	65
18. C	80
19. C	63
20. B	76
21. B	65
22. A	67
23. C	80
24. B	77
25. B	62

RACIAL AND ETHNIC FAMILIES: STRENGTHS AND STRESSES

4

CHAPTER OBJECTIVES

Upon reading Chapter Four students should be able to:

1.   Discuss the various patterns of inter-group relations.

2.   Define and cite examples of minority groups, racial groups, ethnic groups, and racial-ethnic groups.

3.   Discuss the problems of prejudice, discrimination, and racism.

4.   Describe the defining characteristics of African American families.

5.   Describe the defining characteristics of American Indian families.

6.   Describe the defining characteristics of Latino families.

7.   Describe the defining characteristics of Asian American families.

8.   Describe the defining characteristics of Middle Eastern families.

9.   Discuss interracial/interethnic marriages in the U.S. today.

CHAPTER OVERVIEW

U.S. households are increasingly diverse, and the ways that different groups relate to one another is complex. **Assimilation** is the conformity of the ethnic group members to the culture of the dominant group. **Cultural pluralism** is maintaining aspects of one's original culture while living peacefully with the host culture. **Acculturation** involves adopting the language, values, beliefs, roles and other characteristics of the host culture. A **minority group** is a group of people who may be treated differently or unequally because of their physical or cultural characteristics. A **racial group** is a category of people who share physical characteristics, such as skin color, that members of a society consider socially important. An **ethnic group** is a set of people who identify with a common national origin or cultural heritage. A group that has both distinctive racial and cultural characteristics is referred to as a **racial-ethnic group.** Racial-ethnic families face prejudice and discrimination. **Prejudice** is an attitude that prejudges people, usually in a negative way. **Discrimination** is behavior that treats people unequally or unfairly.

African American children are more likely than other racial-ethnic families to grow up with only one parent. Most black families are *egalitarian*, where both men and women share equal authority. Black children are taught to cope with **racism**, a belief that one race is superior to other races. Many black parents engage in **racial socialization**, the process of teaching children to overcome race-related barriers and take pride in their ancestry. The **infant mortality rate** (the number of deaths of babies under 1 year of age per 1,000 live births) among blacks is extremely high. Even more, the median family income is the lowest of all racial-ethnic groups. The strengths of the black family include strong kinship bonds, an ability to adapt family rules, a strong work ethic, determination to succeed in education, and an unwavering spirituality.

American Indians and Alaska Natives make up only 1.5% of the U.S. population. Studies on American Indian families are scarce. American Indian families emphasize values which are very different from those stressed by many in the white community. These include cooperation, sharing, personal integrity, generosity, harmony with nature, and spirituality. American Indian children are taught to respect their elders, and old age is viewed as "*a badge of honor.*" Elders traditionally occupy a central role in family decision making. As families move off of reservations, grandparents serve as "*cultural conservators,*" familiarizing grandchildren with native history. Significant problems that American Indians face are mental health problems, the physical and sexual abuse of children, alcoholism, violence, depression, and suicide. American Indians have consistently been one of the poorest groups in American society. Strengths of the American Indian family include relational bonding, harmony and balance, and spirituality.

Latino men often bear the stereotype of *machismo*, a concept of masculinity that emphasizes dominance, aggression, and womanizing. The positive elements of machismo include courage, honor, *respeto* (respect for authority, tradition and family), *dignidad* (avoiding loss of dignity in front of others), and close ties with the extended family. The female counterpart of machismo is *marianismo*. *Marianismo* expects women to remain virgins until marriage, to be self-sacrificing, and to be unassuming. Even when in the work force, most Latinas devote much of their lives to bearing and rearing children. *Familism,* the idea that family relationships take precedence over individual well being, is common. Being bilingual positively impacts educational attainment. The number of middle class Latino families has increased, yet there is still a high poverty rate. The strengths of the Latino family include resiliency, adaptability, family networks, familism, and ethnic pride.

Female-headed households are less common among Asian Americans than other groups. Many Asian Americans follow Confucianism, which endorses a *patriarchal* structure in which women are taught to obey fathers, husbands, and the oldest son while men serve as heads of the household, principal providers, decision makers, and disciplinarians. In many Asian American families, parents sacrifice personal needs for their children and expect in return *filial piety,* (respect and obedience). The family is more important than the individual, and family solidarity is more important than outside relationships. Asian American families exercise more control over their children's lives than other groups, often using guilt and shame. Educational achievement is stressed. The success of many Asian American families has created a reputation for being the *model minority.* Asian American families have the highest median income. The strengths of the Asian American family include stable households where parents encourage academics and offer personal support that reduces stress against discrimination and leads to better emotional health.

Among those from the Middle East, most children live with both parents, nuclear families are the norm, extended family ties are important, and divorce is frowned upon. Marriage is *endogamous,* favoring marriage between people from the same family or nation. Marriages are often arranged or semi-arranged. Men are socialized to be the family providers and to protect their families, while women take care of the home and children, obey their husbands, and get along with in-laws. Parents reinforce ethnic identity by encouraging their children to associate with peers from their own culture. Middle Eastern families have suffered a larger share of prejudice and discrimination since the 9/11/2001 terrorist attacks. The strengths of Middle Eastern families include biculturalism, ethnic identity, strong family ties, religious beliefs, and extended kin networks.

The young are more accepting of biracial marriages than the old. Laws against *miscegenation* (marriage or sex between people of different races) were outlawed in 1967, in the Supreme Court's *Loving v. Virginia* decision. Interracial and interethnic marriages in the U.S. reflect *exogamy,* marrying outside of one's group. Interracial and interethnic marriages have increased due to proximity, the availability of potential spouses, acculturation, upward mobility, and changing attitudes.

PRE-TEST

1. Your Marriage and Family class takes a trip to Mexico. While there, you notice that your Mexican hosts lump you and your classmates together into one category of people who live in the same country, speak the same language, and prefer the same type of breakfast foods. As Americans, you are a/n:
   a. Racial group
   b. Ethnic group
   c. Racial-ethnic group

2. Tiffany has friends from all racial-ethnic groups, but her parents actively encourage her to associate with peers from her own culture to help strengthen ethnic identity. This practice is common among:
   a. African American families
   b. Middle Eastern families
   c. Latino families

3. Mr. Drummond is a white man that owns an apartment building. His tenants tell him that if he rents an apartment to a black person, they will move out. Although Mr. Drummond loves blacks and has even adopted 2 black sons, he does not allow blacks to move into the building. Mr. Drummond's behavior is an example of:
   a. Prejudice
   b. Discrimination
   c. Racial socialization

4. Escobar is a Latino man. He is raising his son to embrace the positive attributes of machismo. As such, Escobar will teach his son about:
   a. Marianismo
   b. Compadres
   c. Respeto

5. Lisa and Nina are Latina teens. Lisa is bilingual and Nina is not. Research findings suggest that:
   a. Lisa will do better in school
   b. Nina will do better in school
   c. There will be no difference

6. Todd, a white man, tells Pauline, his black wife that they should be ever grateful for the Supreme Court decision that outlawed bans on interracial marriages. Todd appreciates the _____ case.
   a. Roe v. Wade
   b. Plessey v. Ferguson
   c. Loving v. Virginia

7. Gary, an American Indian who lives in the city, visits his grandfather once a month. On these visits, Grandfather takes Gary to participate in reservation activities so that Gary can learn the history of his people. As such, Grandfather is serving as a:
   a. Machismo
   b. Badge of honor
   c. Cultural conservator

8. The racial-ethnic group with the highest median family income is:
   a. Asian Americans
   b. Latinos
   c. African Americans

9. Anisa and her family recently emigrated to the U.S. from Lebanon. While she would have never done so in Lebanon, Anisa wears lipstick and nail polish to school so that she can fit in with her friends. This example of adopting some characteristics of the host culture is:
   a. Acculturation
   b. Cultural Pluralism
   c. Miscegenation

10. Carlita would rather play with her friends, but each day after school she goes to help her grandmother with chores. This idea that family relationships are more important that individual well-being is called:
    a. Familism
    b. Compadrazgo
    c. Machismo

11. Uk Li is an Asian American who knows that his parents have sacrificed a great deal for him. In honor of their sacrifice, Uk Li provides his parents with great respect and obedience. This is called:
    a. Familism
    b. Filial piety
    c. Cultural conservator

12. Milo's father taught him to ignore people that insulted and/or teased him because of his race. Milo's dad was engaging in:
    a. Discrimination
    b. Racial socialization
    c. Prejudice

13. The White Supremacists on campus believe that whites are superior to all other racial groups. This illustrates:
    a. Racial Socialization
    b. Discrimination
    c. Racism

14. Jessica is a newborn baby. Like other children in her racial-ethnic group, Jessica is more likely to be raised by a single parent than a married couple. Jessica is:
    a. Middle Eastern
    b. African American
    c. Latino

15. Raul and his family moved to the U.S. from Cuba. They live in a section of Miami called Little Havana, where Cuban-Americans maintain Cuban cultural traditions. This illustrates:
    a. Acculturation
    b. Cultural Pluralism
    c. Assimilation

16. Leonard is gay. He is treated unequally by members of society because of his sexual orientation. As such, Leonard belongs to a:
    a. Racial group
    b. Ethnic group
    c. Minority group

17. Felix and Diara are an inter-racial couple. They want to move away from that region of the U.S. where interracial couples are most stigmatized. Felix and Diara want to leave the:
    a. West
    b. North
    c. South

18. Oprah Winfrey, Denzel Washington and Whoopi Goldberg all share certain physical characteristics like skin color. This makes them a part of the same:
    a. Racial group
    b. Ethnic group
    c. Both a & b

19. Nat is 70 years old, and his family views his age as a 'badge of honor.' Nat most likely belongs to which group?
    a. American Indian
    b. Middle Eastern
    c. African American

20. Alicia is a Latina teen-ager. She has been taught to remain a virgin until she marries. This is associated with which concept of femininity?
    a. Machismo
    b. Marianismo
    c. Familism

21. Yatou is from Taiwan. She hopes to marry an American man and conform to American culture. This is an example of:
    a. Acculturation
    b. Cultural pluralism
    c. Assimilation

22. The year is 1960. Harry, a white man, wants to marry Bonita, a black woman. However, _____ laws forbid the two from marrying.
    a. Heterogamy
    b. Miscegenation
    c. Exogamy

23. Which racial-ethnic group is LEAST likely to have female-headed homes?
    a. American Indians
    b. African Americans
    c. Asian Americans

24. It is Ashton's birthday and he is turning 10 years old! His parents invite all of the white children from his class to help Ashton celebrate and exclude the minorities. This illustrates:
    a. Prejudice
    b. Discrimination
    c. Racial socialization

25. Tawanna is a black woman who lives in America. To Tawanna, both her physical characteristics and her cultural characteristics are central to her identity. Her physical and cultural characteristics define her:
    a. Racial group
    b. Ethnic group
    c. Racial-ethnic group

APPLICATIONS/EXERCISES

1.   Racial socialization is the process where parents teach children to overcome race-related barriers and take pride in their own ancestry. What types of advice and strategies will you include in the racial socialization of your own children? How is this similar to and/or different from what your parents taught you?

2.   The media portrays more interracial couples than ever before. Think of some of the television shows, movies, and music videos that depict such couples. Which racial-ethnic groups are more likely to be matched together? What messages are being sent concerning interdating?

CHAPTER 4 KEY TERMS CROSSWORD PUZZLE

Across
2. Group sharing physical characteristics
4. Family before self
9. Expects virginity
10. Group sharing cultural heritage
12. Honor and respect to parents
13. Treating people unfairly

Down
1. Expects honor, dignity & respect
3. Conforming to dominant culture
5. Group that is treated unfairly
6. Interracial marriage
7. Infant _____ Rate
8. "Badge of honor"
11. Negative attitude toward certain groups

POST-TEST

1. Otis and Cheryl, like most members of their racial-ethnic group, are an egalitarian couple. They share equal authority. This couple is:
   a. White American
   b. Latino American
   c. African American

2. Manny believes that white teachers know more than black teachers. This illustrates:
   a. Prejudice
   b. Discrimination
   c. Racial socialization

3. The concept of *familism* is most associated with:
   a. American Indians
   b. Latinos
   c. African Americans

4. Kim is expected to obey her father, her husband, and her oldest son. Kim is probably:
   a. Latino
   b. Middle Eastern
   c. Asian American

5. Seven out of every 1,000 babies born in America die. This tells us the _____ rate for the U.S.
   a. Infant morbidity
   b. Infant mortality
   c. Infant survival

6. The racial group with the highest rate of alcohol-related deaths is:
   a. African Americans
   b. Latinos
   c. American Indians

7. Madonna, Tom Hanks, and George Bush all have certain physical characteristics, like skin color in common. As such, they belong to the same:
   a. Ethnic group
   b. Racial group
   c. Both a & b

8. A group of teenagers eat lunch at the park near a group of senior citizens. Which group is more likely to support interracial dating and marriage?
   a. The teens
   b. The senior citizens
   c. They are equally likely

9. Miguel, like many Latino children, is bilingual. Research suggests that being bilingual:
   a. Has a positive effect on academic achievement
   b. Has a negative effect on academic achievement
   c. Has no effect on academic achievement

10. Sam's professor expects him to do well in the class because he belongs to the group known as the model minority. Sam is:
    a. American Indian
    b. Middle Eastern
    c. Asian American

11. Juan is fed up with the way that Latino males are portrayed in the media. Juan wants to see more of the positive traits of machismo. These include:
    a. Marianismo
    b. Familism
    c. Dignidad

12. Barry's family expects him to marry his cousin Shanna. This type of endogamous marriage is most common among _____ families.
    a. Middle Eastern
    b. African American
    c. Latino

13. Melissa needs a new secretary but she will not hire a Hispanic applicant because she believes that all Hispanics steal. This illustrates:
    a. Prejudice
    b. Discrimination
    c. Both a & b

14. The racial-ethnic group with the lowest median family income is:
    a. American Indians
    b. Latinos
    c. African Americans

15. Shema is an African American mother who tells her son that he should be proud of his heritage. She tells him that although he may face discrimination, his ancestors have overcome a great deal. This illustrates:
    a. Familism
    b. Racial socialization
    c. Heterogamy

16. Swan is a Native American who often takes her grandchildren to powwows and tribal hearings. Swan hopes to familiarize her grandchildren with native history. As such, Swan serves as a/an:
    a. Badge of honor
    b. Cultural conservator
    c. Marianismo

17. Marquita recently did an in-class presentation on the Supreme Court's Loving v. Virginia decision. Marquita's report dealt with:
    a. Immigration laws
    b. Laws banning interracial marriage
    c. Discrimination in housing

18. Like most members of their racial-ethnic group, Ty and Tina have never used physical punishment to discipline their children. Instead Ty & Tina use guilt and shame to keep their children in line. Ty and Tina are:
    a. African American
    b. Latino
    c. Asian American

19. Although Rico does not make a whole lot of money, he sends more than ½ of his pay check to his family. In Rico's mind, family relationships take precedence over individual well-being. This illustrates:
    a. Compadrazgo
    b. Machismo
    c. Familism

20. Al and his friends have experienced more prejudice ad discrimination since the September 11, 2001 terrorist attacks. Al and his friends are probably:
    a. Middle Eastern
    b. Asian American
    c. Latino

21. Sambeth and Miyo are a married Asian American couple. They recently sold their home so that they could send their children to the best university in the area. Because of their personal sacrifice, Sambeth and Miyo expect respect and obedience known as:
   a. Familism
   b. Marianismo
   c. Filial piety

22. Bob is a white man who marries Louise, a Latina. This instance of marrying outside of one's group is called:
   a. Exogamy
   b. Endogamy
   c. Pluralism

23. Lola and Roberto are a Hispanic-American couple. They are teaching their daughter to abstain from sex until she is married. They also expect her to be unassuming and self-sacrificial. These are associated with:
   a. Marianismo
   b. Machismo
   c. Familism

24. Aswad and his family moved to the U.S. from the Middle East. As Aswad's philosophy is "When in America, do as the Americans," he has forsaken all of his group's cultural practices to adopt American cultural practices. This illustrates:
   a. Assimilation
   b. Cultural Pluralism
   c. Miscegenation

25. Mr. Wu and his family follow Confucianism. As devout believers, the Wu family is probably:
   a. Patriarchal
   b. Matriarchal
   c. Egalitarian

SELF-ASSESSMENT:
HOW DO YOU VIEW INTERRACIAL RELATIONSHIPS?

Directions: Put a check in the box to reflect whether you agree or disagree with the following statements.

	Agree	Disagree
It is okay for members of my racial group to date outside of our race.		
I would be comfortable introducing my co-workers to my date of a different race.		
I would be comfortable living next door to an interracial couple.		
It is okay for members of different racial groups to pursue relationships with members of my race.		
It is okay for members of my racial group to marry outside of our race.		
I have dated outside of my racial group at least once.		
Interracial relationships are just as likely as same race relationships to survive.		
I would be comfortable introducing my parents to my date of a different race.		
I have dated outside of my racial group more than once.		
The media should portray more interracial couples.		
I would be comfortable if my child married outside of our race.		
I am just as attracted to people of different races as I am to persons within my racial group.		
Interracial dating and marital relationships are good for society.		
I would be comfortable walking in a public place with a date of a different race.		
I would date outside my racial group in the future.		
I would encourage my child to date outside of his/her race.		
I would be comfortable introducing my friends of a different race.		

Key: Give yourself 1 point for every statement that you checked as 'Agree.' A score of 17 represents the most accepting views toward interracial relationships. A score of 0 represents opposition to interracial relations.

ANSWERS

PRE-TEST

Answers	Page Numbers
1. B	90
2. B	110
3. B	91
4. C	101
5. A	102
6. C	113
7. C	99
8. A	107
9. A	86
10. A	102
11. B	105
12. B	94
13. C	94
14. B	92
15. B	86
16. C	89
17. C	113
18. A	90
19. A	99
20. B	101
21. C	86
22. B	113
23. C	105
24. B	91
25. C	90

KEY TERMS CROSSWORD PUZZLE

Across	Page Numbers
2. Racial	90
4. Familism	102
9. Marianismo	102
10. Ethnic	90
12. Filial piety	105
13. Discrimination	91
Down	
1. Machismo	102
3. Assimilation	86
5. Minority	89
6. Miscegenation	113
7. Mortality	95
8. Old Age	99
11. Prejudice	91

POST-TEST

Answers	Page Numbers
1. C	92
2. A	91
3. B	102
4. C	105
5. B	95
6. C	99
7. B	90
8. A	113
9. A	102
10. C	107
11. C	101
12. A	110
13. C	91
14. C	95
15. B	94
16. B	99
17. B	113
18. C	106
19. C	102
20. A	111
21. C	105
22. A	113
23. A	102
24. A	86
25. A	105

5

SOCIALIZATION AND GENDER ROLES

CHAPTER OBJECTIVES

Upon reading Chapter Five, students should be able to:

1. Compare and contrast sex and gender.

2. Discuss the nature-nurture debate.

3. Explain the three main theories of socialization.

4. Describe the primary sources of socialization for children.

5. Discuss traditional gender roles.

6. Describe how gender roles impact various areas of adult life.

7. Describe gender-role changes and constraints.

8. Discuss cross-cultural variations in gender role identity.

CHAPTER OVERVIEW

Sex and gender are related but not the same. **Sex** refers to the biological characteristics with which we are born and is based on physical traits. **Gender** consists of learned attitudes and behaviors that characterize a given sex and is based on social and cultural expectations. **Gender roles** are the characteristics, attitudes, feelings, and behaviors that society expects of males and females. *Gendered* refers to the process of treating and evaluating males and females differently because of their sex. **Gender identity**, a person's perception of self as either masculine or feminine, develops early in life. *The nature-nurture* debate refers to the difference in opinion among social scientists concerning whether gender roles are learned and due to the environment or are innate and due to heredity. Scientists believe that **hormones**, chemical substances secreted into the bloodstream, explain some of the differences between males and females. All males and females share the hormones *estrogen* (dominant in women and produced in the ovaries), *progesterone* (present in high levels during pregnancy and secreted by the ovaries) and *testosterone* (dominant in males and produced by the testes). **Transgendered** is an umbrella term for people who adopt a gender identity that differs from their sex at birth. *Transvestites* dress in clothing of the opposite sex. **Transsexuals** are people who feel that their gender identity is out of sync with their anatomical sex. Males are more likely to be violent in a **patriarchy** (men hold the positions of power and authority) than in a **matriarchy** (women hold the positions of power and control). *Hermaphrodites* or *intersexuals* are people born with male and female sex organs. Parents of such infants usually choose a sex for the child and use hormones and surgery to change the genital organs.

There are three major perspectives that explain how gender roles are learned. **Social-learning theory** suggests that people learn attitudes, beliefs, and behaviors through social interaction. Learning occurs through *reinforcement* (rewards and punishments), imitation (watching who does what in the family), and *role models* (parents, celebrities, etc.). **Cognitive-development theory** argues that children acquire female or male values on their own by thinking, reasoning, and interpreting information in their environment. Children pass through developmental and after acquiring masculine or feminine traits, the child tends to identify with people of the same-sex. During adolescence many youth conform to **gender-role stereotypes**, the belief and expectation that people will act according to traditional gender roles. **Feminist theories** suggest that gender is a social role that is taught carefully and repeatedly; *gender scripts* (how society expects people to act based on sex) lead to inequalities; and behavior will change when traditional roles for men and women change.

We learn gender from a variety of sources. Parents are typically the first and most influential socializing agent. Parents influence their children's gender by talking differently with, setting different expectations for, and providing different opportunities to boys and girls. Toys influence the gender of children because toy stores divide goods by sex, and play is typically sex-typed. Sports shape gender as boys are more likely than girls to participate in sports and females have fewer athletic roles models. Peers influence gender roles by offering gender-typed play. Teachers and schools deliver gender related messages to children, giving boys more attention, providing girls with more help, and expecting girls to be neat, polite, and well-groomed. Books and textbooks often reinforce sex-stereotypical images of women and men. Popular culture and the media reinforce sex stereotyping from childhood to adulthood in advertising, newspapers, magazines, television, and music videos. Religion shapes gender roles because it provides divinely ordained responsibilities for both sexes.

Traditionally, males are *instrumental* (procreator, protector, and provider) and women are *expressive* (emotional support and nurturing qualities that sustain the family unit and support the husband/father). Traditional gender roles have both benefits and costs. On the positive side, traditional gender roles promote stability, continuity, and predictability. On the negative side, they can create economic pressure, exhaustion, boredom, and loneliness. Traditional gender roles persist because they are profitable for business and they maintain male privilege and power. Women spend more time than men on family care tasks. Many women take on the *second shift*, household work and childcare that mothers face after coming home from work. Inequities in the workplace include sex discrimination and sexual harassment. The *glass ceiling* is an unofficial and discriminatory barrier that limits women's chances of rising to positions of power and responsibility. **Sexual harassment** is any unwelcome sexual advance, request for sexual favors, or conduct of a sexual nature that makes a person feel uncomfortable and interferes with his/her work. The 1986 Supreme Court case of *Meritor Savings Bank v. Vinson* ruled that sexual harassment violates federal antidiscrimitaion laws. Research demonstrates that women and men have distinctive communication styles that include different purposes, different rules, and different ways of interpreting communications.

As gender roles change, most people will encounter **role conflict**, the frustration and uncertainties a person experiences when confronted with the requirements of two or more roles that are incompatible with each other. Androgyny, which allows people to play both instrumental and expressive roles, may be the solution to sexist gender roles. The degree of equality between men and women differs across societies. The *Gender Development Index* (GDI) measures the status and quality of life of women using life expectancy, educational attainment, and income. The lowest ranked countries are in Africa.

PRE-TEST

1. Myra is a business executive who is a single parent. She is the protector and provider of her children. Also, she serves as their nurturing supporter. Being both instrumental and expressive, Myra illustrates:
   a. Sex
   b. Androgyny
   c. Patriarchy

2. In sex education class today, Mrs. Hawkins taught her teen-aged students that chemical substances were being excreted into their bloodstreams, producing different physiological changes. Mrs. Hawkins taught her students about:
   a. Genes
   b. Chromosomes
   c. Hormones

3. Rebecca has taken a job at a company that is known to ignore sexual harassment. Rebecca meets with the Human Resources manager and cites the Supreme Court ruling of sexual harassment as anti-discriminatory. Rebecca cites:
   a. Meritor Savings Bank v. Vinson
   b. Loving v. Virginia
   c. Roe v. Wade

4. Dr. Price teaches a parenting class. She tells the parents that providing rewards and punishments for gender role behavior is a good way to shape children's behavior. Dr. Price subscribes to:
   a. Social learning theory
   b. Cognitive development theory
   c. Feminist theory

5. When Elias hears his older brother being called a 'sissy' for taking ballet classes, Elias decides that he will never take dance class. According to social learning theory, this illustrates:
   a. Reinforcement
   b. Imitation
   c. Modeling

6. For the past week, Darren has sent his colleague Samantha a note each day requesting different sexual favors. Samantha is visibly upset and unable to effectively do her job. This illustrates:
   a. Sexual discrimination
   b. Sexual harassment
   c. Sexual scripting

7. Nisha hates the traditional gender roles, and she wants to understand why they persist. After reading her textbook, Nisha realizes that _____ make money because of traditional gender roles.
   a. Women
   b. Child care workers
   c. Businesses

8. Marcus suggests that society's expectations based on sex contribute to inequality in society. Marcus subscribes to:
   a. Social learning theory
   b. Cognitive development theory
   c. Feminist theory

9. Natalie is a partner at a prestigious law firm. She works 80 hours per week and spends only about 2 hours per week with her three children. By failing to be expressive, Natalie is violating:
   a. Hormones
   b. Gender roles
   c. Sexual scripts

10. Kiyo is a student at the college and a cashier at the local convenience store. Kiyo needs to study for exams but she also needs to work so that she can pay her bills. The frustration that Kiyo experiences as she faces the requirements of two different roles is called:
   a. Role strain
   b. Role conflict
   c. Role socialization

11. Bob is a terrific husband! He is a great procreator, provider, and protector. As such, Bob is:
   a. Instrumental
   b. Expressive
   c. Both a & b

12. The eleven countries where women have the worst life expectancy, educational attainment, and income are all in:
   a. Africa
   b. The Middle East
   c. Asia

13. Ruth teaches 7th grade English. After work each day, Ruth goes home to cook, clean, and help the children with their homework. This illustrates the:
   a. Double shift
   b. Second shift
   c. Expressive shift

14. Carol, who has raised seven children, gives advice to her neighbor on childrearing. Carol says, "Children go through different stages in becoming masculine or feminine." Which theory of gender socialization does this match?
    a. Social learning theory
    b. Cognitive development theory
    c. Feminist theory

15. Jamaal wants to know about the quality of life for women around the world. Jamaal's teacher advises him to check out the:
    a. Gender Development Index (GDI)
    b. Gender Role Monitor (GRM)
    c. Women's Rights Ruler (WRR)

16. Abraham often tells his friends about the high rate of male violence and aggression in his native land. Based on this information, Abraham's native country is probably:
    a. Patriarchal
    b. Matriarchal
    c. Egalitarian

17. Over a light lunch at the country club, Paul told his friends that he would only allow women to work as senior managers at his firm. Paul said that he would never promote a woman to the vice-presidency. Paul is revealing a discriminatory barrier known as:
    a. Sexual harassment
    b. Sexual scripting
    c. The glass ceiling

18. Tony was born a male but now lives life as a female. Tony is:
    a. Gendered
    b. Transgendered
    c. Gender scripted

19. Drs. Turner and Hooch are discussing the reasons that men and women are different. Dr. Turner argues that it is because of biology while Dr. Hooch posits that it is because of environment. This illustrates the:
    a. Biological-sociological debate
    b. Turner-Hooch debate
    c. Nature-nurture debate

20. _____ is based on biology while _____ is based on cultural expectations.
    a. Sex, Gender
    b. Gender, sex
    c. None of the above

21. Every morning, Pete watches his father shave. Pete looks forward to the day when he will be able to do so. This illustrates:
    a. Scripting
    b. Reinforcement
    c. Imitation

22. Renee just found out that she is pregnant. Over the next few months, Renee's body will produce _____ in high levels.
    a. Testosterone
    b. Progesterone
    c. Estrogen

23. Tamika dreams of a world where women are the leaders in politics and the economy. The society that Tamika dreams of is:
    a. Patriarchal
    b. Matriarchal
    c. Egalitarian

24. In the Thompson family, the males mow the lawn and take out the trash, and the females wash the dishes and do the laundry. This family is:
    a. Transgendered
    b. Gendered
    c. Transexual

25. Ted is a 'man's man'. He likes to fix cars, fish, and hunt. Ted sees himself as very masculine. This illustrates Ted's:
    a. Gender identity
    b. Gender role
    c. Gender script

APPLICATIONS/EXERCISES

1. Consider your gender role. What influence did your parents, teachers, books, popular culture, peers, and religion have on your gender socialization.

2. Think back on how you have responded to your male and female friends who violated society's gender expectations. In which cases did you show the most disapproval? Why?

CHAPTER 5 KEY TERMS CROSSWORD PUZZLE

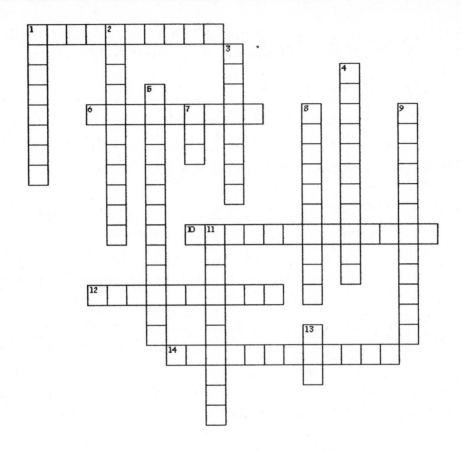

Across

1. Unwanted sexual advances at work
6. Expressive plus instrumental
10. Rewards and punishments
12. Where women are in charge
14. Role for the provider

Down

1. Chemical substances in bloodstream
2. Women's work after work
3. Gender perception of self
4. Cognitive _____ Theory
5. Gender ID different now
7. Measures status of women
8. Where men rule
9. Demands from 2 roles
11. Role for the nurturer
13. Biological Characteristics

POST-TEST

1. Marilyn likes pink, plays with dolls, and loves to dress in frilly skirts. She sees herself as very feminine. This refers to Marilyn's:
   a. Gender role
   b. Gender identity
   c. Gender script

2. Sue believes that it is a man's world. Men are the major decision makers in families and at work. This type of society is:
   a. Patriarchal
   b. Matriarchal
   c. Egalitarian

3. Isaac feels that he is trapped in the wrong body. Although he was born a male, Isaac believes that he should have been born a female. Isaac is:
   a. Transsexual
   b. Gendered
   c. Gender scripted

4. Dr. Monroe maintains that culture or environment shapes gender behavior. Dr. Monroe is most likely:
   a. A social scientist
   b. A biologist
   c. Transgendered

5. In biology class today Gerald learned about the chemical substances that are secreted into the bloodstream. Gerald had a lesson on:
   a. Chromosomes
   b. Hormones
   c. Genetics

6. Although Bill has always enjoyed playing in tea parties with his sister, at the age of 5 Bill is at the stage in which he avoids opposite-sex toys. This supports which theory?
   a. Cognitive development theory
   b. Social learning theory
   c. Feminist theory

7. Every morning, Blair watches her mother put on make-up. Blair believes that all women should wear make-up, and she looks forward to the day when she will be able to do so. This illustrates:
   a. Scripting
   b. Reinforcement
   c. Imitation

8. Pat was born as a female but now lives as a male. Pat is:
   a. Gendered
   b. Transgendered
   c. Gender scripted

9. After summer vacation, Mickey returns to campus buff and muscular. His friends joke that Mickey's _____ hormones, which are responsible for strengthening muscle, have been working overtime.
   a. Estrogen
   b. Progesterone
   c. Testosterone

10. On the first day at the new job, Walter had to watch a video on sexual harassment. The video discussed the Supreme Court case which ruled that sexual harassment is a violation of antidiscrimination laws. That case was:
    a. Loving v. Virginia
    b. Roe v. Wade
    c. Meritor Savings Bank v. Vinson

11. In Zilla's native country, there is a high rate of male violence and aggression. Based on research, Zilla's country of origin is probably:
    a. Patriarchal
    b. Matriarchal
    c. Egalitarian

12. When Ayesha is called a tomboy because she climbs a tree with her cousins, she realizes that girls are not supposed to climb trees. According to social learning theory, this illustrates:
    a. Reinforcement
    b. Imitation
    c. Modeling

13. Michelle believes that because of sex discrimination she will never be promoted beyond middle management by her present employer. This illustrates:
    a. Sexual harassment
    b. The glass ceiling
    c. Sexual scripting

14. Rachel is a warm and sympathetic wife/mother who provides emotional support for her family. Rachel is fulfilling the:
    a. Expressive role
    b. Instrumental role
    c. Both a & b

15. Tommy and Gail are a married couple who share equally in the instrumental and expressive tasks to set an example for their children. They believe that if the traditional gender roles change, behavior will also change. Tommy and Gail subscribe to:
    a. Social learning theory
    b. Cognitive development theory
    c. Feminist theory

16. Kerry is a legal secretary, and her husband Doug is a deliveryman. They both work eight hour shifts, but when Kerry gets home she prepares dinner, irons clothes, and cleans the house. Kerry tells Doug that she is tired of working the:
    a. Second shift
    b. Expressive shift
    c. Double shift

17. The most influential agent of gender socialization is:
    a. Toys
    b. Media
    c. Parents

18. Which of the following is true?
    a. Women and men are equally likely to care for the home and children
    b. Women are more likely than men to care for the home and children
    c. Men are more likely than women to care for the home and children

19. Alex is a hard working business owner who loves to spend time nurturing his children. This blend of the instrumental and expressive is called:
    a. Androgyny
    b. Gendered
    c. Hermaphrodite

20. Mr. Wright touches his secretary's leg whenever he walks by her. This unwanted sexual advance interferes with the secretary's ability to do her work. This is an example of:
    a. Sexual scripting
    b. Sexual harassment
    c. Sexual discrimination

21. GDI refers to:
    a. Gender Development Index
    b. Gender Drug Investigation
    c. Gender Doesn't Intimidate

22. Lee was born with both male and female sex organs. Lee is a:
    a. transsexual
    b. homosexual
    c. hermaphrodite

23. Alvin would love to be a stay-at-home dad. Yet, he feels that making this choice would be a violation of _____, the behavior that society expects of him.
    a. Hormones
    b. Gender roles
    c. Androgyny

24. Jeff is a father and an architect. Jeff's daughter is having her first dance recital tonight. However, Jeff's boss has asked him to stay late at work to finish the project they have been working on. This frustration of facing the requirements of two different incompatible roles is called:
    a. Role conflict
    b. Role strain
    c. Role socialization

25. Which of the following is true?
    a. Young children prefer same-sex play partners.
    b. Young children prefer opposite sex play partners.
    c. Young children have no preference in the sex of their play partners

SELF-ASSESSMENT:
HOW ANDROGYNOUS ARE YOU?

Directions: Circle the two words from each row that best describe you.

	Column 1	Column 2	Column 3	Column 4
Row 1	Aggressive	Sensitive	Athletic	Nurturing
Row 2	Tough	Passive	Loud	Emotional
Row 3	Brave	Gentle	Ambitious	Homebody
Row 4	Independent	Considerate	Demanding	Moody
Row 5	Untidy	Warm	Impatient	Graceful
Row 6	Strong	Submissive	Rational	Beautiful
Row 7	Leader	Caregiver	Forceful	Obedient
Row 8	Dominant	Homemaker	Assertive	Child-Lover
Row 9	Stubborn	Artsy	Calm	Stylish
Row 10	Active	Neat	Domineering	Sympathetic
Row 11	Provider	Thoughtful	Outdoorsy	Needy
Row 12	Breadwinner	Sexy	Risk-taker	Sweet
Row 13	Flexible	Supportive	Confident	Shy
Row 14	Adventurous	Talkative	Protector	Innocent
Row 15	Rowdy	Patient	Handsome	Expressive

Key: Give yourself 1 point for every word that you circled in Column 1 and 1 point for every word that you circled in Column 3. Tally up you score.

- 0-3   Extremely Feminine
- 4-9   Feminine
- 10-13   Somewhat Feminine
- 14-16   Extremely Androgynous
- 17-20   Somewhat Masculine
- 21-26   Masculine
- 27-30   Extremely Masculine

Does this assessment match your gender identity? Why or why not?

ANSWERS

PRE-TEST

Answers	Page Numbers
1. B	149
2. C	122
3. A	144
4. A	128
5. A	128
6. B	144
7. C	140
8. C	129
9. B	121
10. B	146
11. A	139
12. A	151
13. B	142
14. B	129
15. A	149
16. A	125
17. C	144
18. B	123
19. C	122
20. A	121
21. C	128
22. B	122
23. B	
24. B	
25. A	

KEY TERMS CROSSWORD PUZZLE

Across	Page Numbers
1. Harassment	144
6. Androgyny	149
10. Reinforcement	128
12. Matriarchy	126
14. Instrumental	139

Down	
1. Hormones	122
2. Second Shift	142
3. Identity	121
4. Development	129
5. Transgendered	123
7. GDI	149
8. Patriarchy	125
9. Role Conflict	146
11. Expressive	139
13. Sex	121

POST-TEST

Answers	Page Numbers
1. B	127
2. A	126
3. A	123
4. A	122
5. B	122
6. A	129
7. A	128
8. B	123
9. C	122
10. C	144
11. A	125
12. A	128
13. B	149
14. A	139
15. C	129
16. A	142
17. C	130
18. B	142
19. A	149
20. B	144
21. A	149
22. C	126
23. B	121
24. A	146
25. A	132

6

LOVE AND LOVING RELATIONSHIPS

CHAPTER OBJECTIVES

Upon reading Chapter Six, students should be able to:

1. Explain the importance of self love.

2. Describe the qualities needed for friendship and love.

3. Discuss the characteristics of love.

4. Compare and contrast sexual arousal and sexual desire.

5. Discuss caring, intimacy, and commitment.

6. Explain the theories of love and loving.

7. Explain the functions of love.

8. Describe gender differences in love.

9. Compare and contrast the experience of love by sexual orientation.

10. Describe the barriers to experiencing love.

11. Discuss the factors that disrupt loving relationships.

12. Compare and contrast romantic love and long-term love.

13. Discuss cross-cultural variations in love.

CHAPTER OVERVIEW

Love is essential for human survival. Love for oneself, or self-love, is necessary for our social and emotional development. There are eight important qualities in friendship: enjoyment, acceptance, trust, respect, mutual support, confiding, understanding, and honesty. Love includes all of these qualities plus sexual desire, priority over other relationships, and caring to the point of self-sacrifice. It is unlikely that a person can love someone who is not a friend. Love is multi-faceted, based on respect and often demanding. Societal and group practices and expectations shape romantic experiences. All societies have rules about *homogamy* (dating within one's group) and *exogamy* (marrying someone outside the group). S*exual arousal* (physiological response that may occur consciously or unconsciously) differs from *sexual desire* (psychological state in which a person wants to obtain a sexual object or engage in a sexual activity). Healthy loving relationships include *caring* (the desire to help another by providing aid and support), *intimacy* (feelings of closeness), and commitment (the intent to remain in a relationship). There are 3 types of intimacy: *physical* (sex, hugging, touching), *affective* (feeling close) and *verbal* (self disclosure). **Self disclosure** involves revealing honest thoughts and feelings to another person.

Biological perspectives argue that love is grounded in evolution, biology, and chemistry in that romance draws people into child-producing partnerships as natural amphetamines cause feelings of romantic-love. *Endorphins*, chemicals like morphine that reside in the brain, have a calming effect that sustains long-term relationships. *Sociological perspectives* claim that culture is the force behind love. **Attachment theory** holds that the primary motivation in life is to be connected with other people and that there are three attachment styles: *secure* (trusts romantic partners and is confident of partner's love), *anxious/ambivalent* (falls in love immediately and wants a commitment fast) and *avoidant* (has little trust for others, cynical beliefs about love and is unable to handle intimacy). Reiss's wheel theory of love describes four stages of love *(rapport self-revelation, mutual dependency*, and *personality need fulfillment)*, which turn like spokes on a wheel. Sternberg's triangular theory of love outlines the components of love as three elements of a triangle: *intimacy* (closeness), *passion* (romance, physical attraction, and sex) and *decision commitment* (decision to love and commitment to maintain love). Love varies in its mix of the components. John Lee suggested that there are six styles of love: **eros** (love of beauty), **mania** (obsessive love), **ludus** (playful love), **storge** (companionate love), **agape** (self-sacrificing love), and **pragma** (practical love). *Exchange theory* explains that love relationships involve social exchanges that provide costs and rewards to each person. If initial interactions are reciprocal and mutually satisfying, a relationship continues; but if needs are mismatched, love interests may decline.

Love, in fulfilling many functions, ensures human survival, prolongs life, enhances physical health, improves quality of life, and offers fun. There are gender differences in love. Men are more romantic than women and males and females differ in their styles of showing affection. The *feminization of love* involves excluding the instrumental and physical ways that men show affection. **Homophobia,** the fear and hatred of homosexuals, has decreased in the last decade. As such, lesbians and gay men are more likely admit that they are lovers. Homosexual and heterosexual love is similar. In both types, partners want to be emotionally close, expect faithfulness, plan to grow old together, and experience painful break-ups. One major difference is that lesbians and gay men are criticized for public displays of affection. The barriers to experiencing love include: mass society, demographic variables, double standards, selfish individualism, and family/personality characteristics.

Some behaviors are hazardous to loving relationships. *Narcissists* are people who have exaggerated feelings of power and self-importance. To maintain dominance, narcissists tend to play games. *Jealousy* occurs when people believe that a rival is competing for a lover's affection. Jealous people tend to depend more heavily on their partners for their self-esteem, consider themselves inadequate as mates, and feel that they are more deeply involved than their partners. *Evolutionary psychologists* suggest that men are more jealous of women's sexual infidelity while women are more jealous of their partner's emotional entanglements. Jealousy may lead to stalking or *cyberstalking* (threatening or unwanted advances involving electronic communication). Unhealthy, controlling behavior in love relationships also includes pressuring the partner to prove his/her love, using guilt to justify actions, emotional abuse, and physical abuse. Unrequited love occurs when one does not return another's romantic feelings.

There are significant differences between romantic love, which thrives on beliefs about love at first sight and fate, and long-term love, which provides security and constancy. Romantic love is simple whereas lasting love is more complicated; romantic love is self-centered, whereas long-term love is altruistic; romantic love is short-lived whereas long-term love grows and develops; romantic love is ludic whereas long-term love is storgic. Long-term love increases socio-economic status.

Expressing love varies across countries and cultures. In Western societies that emphasize individualism, love may or may not lead to marriage. In cultures that stress group and community, arrangements between families are more important than romantic love. In many Western countries, people become engaged and then inform family and friends. In other countries, **arranged marriage**, in which parents or relatives choose a person's partner, is common. In such arrangements, it is expected that love will grow over time. Arranged marriages persist because they offer stability and family ties.

PRE-TEST

1. Mallory tells Jeff that it really bothers her when he makes fun of her cooking in front of the children. By revealing her honest thoughts and feelings, Mallory is engaging in:
   a. Narcissism
   b. Jealousy
   c. Self-disclosure

2. Thiaba and Ibrahima are not in love. They are getting married tomorrow because their families have selected them for one another. Their marriage is:
   a. Forced
   b. Arranged
   c. Contemporary

3. Sotori has a self-sacrificing love for Amoko. He would give her the shirt off of his back. This illustrates _____ love:
   a. Agape
   b. Pragma
   c. Ludus

4. Grady loves Wendy and he expresses it by washing her car and changing her oil. Wendy does not view these instrumental tasks as an expression of love. This illustrates the:
   a. Feminization of love
   b. Exchange theory
   c. Narcissist idea

5. Naomi says, "In my marriage I give, give, give, and my husband Vinton just takes, takes, takes!" Which theory suggests that this marriage will end because it is not mutually satisfying?
   a. Attachment
   b. Reiss' Wheel Theory of Love
   c. Exchange Theory

6. Her friends notice that Sheila falls in love quickly and wants commitment immediately. Sheila's attachment style is:
   a. Avoidant
   b. Secure
   c. Anxious/ambivalent

7. Which of the following is true?
   a. Men are more romantic than women.
   b. Women are more romantic than men.
   c. Men and women are equal in romance.

8. Whenever Will walks by Tyra's cubicle, she thinks about caressing his body and kissing his lips. This illustrates:
    a. Sexual desire
    b. Sexual arousal
    c. Both a & b

9. Fred and Wilma have been married for fifteen years. The fact that both feel comfortable and secure in their marriage is attributed to which chemicals in the brain:
    a. PEA
    b. Endorphins
    c. Amphetamines

10. Sara has sex for fun, not emotional support. She has several partners but is afraid of commitment. Sara tells her friends that she just wants to "Hit it and quit it." This playful style of love is:
    a. Mania
    b. Ludus
    c. Agape

11. Laura loves George because he is a provider and a protector. This practical form of love is:
    a. Agape
    b. Pragma
    c. Storge

12. Hillary sees herself as superior to her husband Bill and constantly tries to steal the spotlight away from him. Hillary is:
    a. A cyberstalker
    b. Jealous
    c. A Narcissist

13. Perfumes that are made with the natural scent of humans in an effort to spark physical attraction are based on the _____ perspective of love:
    a. Sociological
    b. Biological
    c. Both a & b

14. Abdul does not trust other people and will not allow his girlfriend to get too close to him. According to attachment theory, Abdul is:
    a. Anxious/ambivalent
    b. Avoidant
    c. Secure

15. Enrique and Lola are equally passionate, intimate, and committed. Which theory would suggest that the two are perfectly matched?
    a. Triangular theory of love
    b. Social exchange
    c. Attachment

16. Brad just received a football scholarship to the state university. Brad's girlfriend Tracy is disappointed. She believes that once Brad becomes a star college football player, he will not want her anymore. Tracy is experiencing:
    a. Narcissism
    b. Jealousy
    c. Self-disclosure

17. Kara is away at college. Every week her parents send her a care package of food, clothes, and gift cards because they want to help her. This illustrates:
    a. Caring
    b. Intimacy
    c. Commitment

18. Geraldine watches a movie which portrays a fear and hatred of homosexuals. The movie depicts:
    a. Homophobia
    b. Endorphins
    c. Narcissism

19. Tia and Tamara are twin sisters and best friends. They have a closeness which involves hugging and sharing their deepest thoughts. This illustrates:
    a. Commitment
    b. Caring
    c. Intimacy

20. Which of the following is true?
    a. Women are more jealous of their partner's sexual infidelity than men
    b. Men are more jealous of their partner's sexual infidelity than women
    c. Men and women are equally jealous of their partner's sexual infidelity

21. Tomas has been sending unwanted sexual advances to Carmen's email box. This illustrates:
    a. Jealousy
    b. Narcissism
    c. Cyberstalking

22. Sandy and Danny experienced love at first sight. This is also called:
    a. Agape love
    b. Storge love
    c. Eros love

23. Emmanuel makes a list of his priorities and realizes that his most important goal in life is to connect with other people. This supports:
    a. The triangular theory of love
    b. Reiss's wheel theory of love
    c. The attachment theory

24. Darren loves Samantha but Samantha does not love Darren. This is _____ love.
    a. Unrequited
    b. Wasted
    c. Jealous

25. Terrell is in the 6th grade. His teacher tells him to go and write his answer on the board, but Terrell does not want to leave his seat because he has an erection. Terrell is experiencing:
    a. Sexual arousal
    b. Sexual desire
    c. Both a & b

APPLICATIONS/EXERCISES

1. Think about the lyrics of your favorite love song. What attachment styles (attachment theory), style of love (Lee), components of love (triangular theory) and stages (Reiss' Wheel theory of Love) are apparent?

2. Consider your single friends and family members that want a mate but just have not found one yet. Which barriers to love are in operation?

CHAPTER 6 KEY TERMS CROSSWORD PUZZLE

Across
1. Adult with warm parents
4. Companionate love
5. Sexual response by the body
6. Sacrificial love
9. Self-important person
12. Obsessive love
13. Playful love
14. Marriage set up by parents

Down
2. Unwanted advances via e-mail
3. Fear and hatred of gays
7. Practical love
8. Adults who can't handle intimacy
10. Closeness
11. Love at 1st sight
15. Sexual response in the mind

POST-TEST

1. Wayne and Cherie have been married for seven months. Wayne tells Cherie that he is meeting his ex-girlfriend, who is in town for the weekend, for dinner. Cherie believes that Wayne's ex-girlfriend is a threat to their relationship. Cherie is experiencing:
   a. Narcissism
   b. Jealousy
   c. Self-Disclosure

2. Jethro is a single man that wants a wife. Jethro's uncle Jed does not understand why an attractive young man like Jethro is still single. Jethro explains that opportunities to meet women in person have declined because of:
   a. Demographics
   b. Individualism
   c. Mass society

3. Boris, who believes that he is God's gift to women, has grandiose feelings of power and self importance. This makes Boris:
   a. Jealous
   b. A Narcissist
   c. A Stalker

4. At their wedding, Monica and Chandler stated that they would remain together through sickness and health, as well as wealth and poverty. This intent to stay together is called:
   a. Intimacy
   b. Commitment
   c. Caring

5. Reggie lists the rewards and costs of staying with his girlfriend. Reggie examines his list and notices that he is getting just as much as he is giving. Which theory suggests that Reggie will continue the relationship?
   a. Reiss' Wheel Theory of Love
   b. Attachment Theory
   c. Exchange Theory

6. Rahab is obsessive, possessive, and jealous. She frequently drives by her boyfriend's house when he does not answer his phone. This style of love is:
   a. Agape
   b. Storge
   c. Mania

7. Tank has a fun and games approach to dating. His philosophy of love is, "Get in, Get up, Get out!" This playful style of love is:
   a. Mania
   b. Ludus
   c. Storge

8. At their 50th wedding anniversary, Myrtle was asked to talk about her marriage to Harry. Myrtle said that she noticed her relationship going through four different stages over and over again. This supports:
   a. Reiss' wheel theory of love
   b. Attachment theory
   c. Triangular theory of love

9. Brian believes that culture, not biology, led him to his wife Maresha. Brian's beliefs support the:
   a. Sociological perspective
   b. Biological perspective
   c. Both a &b

10. Which of the following is true?
    a. Men are more jealous of their partner's emotional infidelity than women
    b. Women are more jealous of their partner's emotional infidelity than men
    c. Men and women are equally jealous of their partner's emotional infidelity

11. Rebecca wants her husband to hug her, kiss her, and tell her he loves her. He does that sometimes, but more often he expresses his love by washing her car and carrying her bags. Rebecca discounts these expressions and insists that he express his love in the way that she likes. This is known as:
    a. Narcissism
    b. The feminization of love
    c. Jealousy

12. The lyrics of a popular song say, "You had me from hello." The songwriter is referring to love based on physical attraction or
    a. Eros love
    b. Mania love
    c. Ludus love

13. When Phillip sees Vivian, his breath quickens, his palms sweat, and his skin flushes. This physiological response illustrates:
   a. Sexual desire
   b. Sexual arousal
   c. Both a & b

14. Bonnie wants more intimacy than Clyde, and Clyde wants more passion than Bonnie. Which theory which suggest that the two are mismatched?
   a. Attachment theory
   b. Triangular theory of love
   c. Exchange theory

15. Dorothy and Stanley visited Albania to find a wife for their son, Michael. Michael will accept his parent's choice without question. This illustrates:
   a. The guilt trip
   b. Arranged marriage
   c. Narcissism

16. When the burglar pointed the gun at his wife, Patrick jumped in front of her to protect her. In being willing to sacrifice his own life for his wife, Patrick demonstrated _____ love.
   a. Pragma
   b. Agape
   c. Ludus

17. Michael caught Rebecca cheating. He responded by restating his intent to stay with her and work through their problems. This illustrates:
   a. Caring
   b. Intimacy
   c. Commitment

18. Barney and Betty often exchange jokes, sexual desires, and ideas. Reiss's wheel theory of love suggests the couple is in the ____ stage:
   a. Rapport
   b. Self-revelation
   c. Mutual dependency

19. Jason and Maggie have an affectionate love that has developed over 17 years and four children. This style of love is:
   a. Ludus
   b. Storge
   c. Agape

20. Muhammad had warm and supportive parents. He trusts his wife and is confident that she loves him. Muhammad is:
a. Secure
b. Anxious/ambivalent
c. Avoidant

21. Maya knows exactly what she wants in a man. In fact, she made a list of the characteristics that are desirable: protector, provider, procreator. Maya wants a love that is based on practicality. This is:
a. Pragma
b. Eros
c. Agape

22. Which type of relationship is associated with higher socio-economic levels?
a. Romantic love
b. Arranged marriage
c. Long-term love

23. At a 5th grade social studies bee, the children are asked if arranged marriages or love-based marriages are more common in the world today. The correct answer is:
a. Arranged marriage
b. Love-based marriage
c. There is no difference in the prevalence of arranged and love-based marriage

24. Omar tells his girlfriend about his phobia, or fear of spiders. This revelation of his thoughts and feelings is an example of:
a. Narcissism
b. Self-disclosure
c. Homophobia

25. Before Marty learned that his eldest son was gay, he had a fear and hatred of homosexuals. Back then, Marty was:
a. Narcissistic
b. Homophobic
c. Jealous

SELF-ASSESSMENT:
HOW JEALOUS ARE YOU?

Directions: Read each statement. Put a check in the box to reflect whether or not you would be upset if faced with the scenario.

	Upset	Not Upset
Your mate compliments your friend but does not compliment you.		
Your mate is going on a cruise with his/her friends for spring break and you were not invited.		
Your mate is meeting an ex-mate for coffee.		
Your mate has a new friend and is spending an increasing amount of time with the newcomer.		
Your mate cancels a date with you to study for a final exam.		
Your mate makes comments about how attractive another person is.		
Your mate is late picking you because he/she was hanging out with friends.		
Your mate is spending more and more time on his/her favorite hobby.		
Your mate visits your home and spends most of his/her time with your roommate.		
Your mate cancels a date with you to visit a friend in the hospital.		
Your mate has a makeover and looks HOT!		
Your mate takes a call on a cell phone while you are together.		
Your mate visits family members every day after work.		
Your mate purchases an expensive gift for a friend.		
Your mate gets off the phone with you to talk with someone else.		

Key: Give yourself 1 point for every statement that you checked as 'Upset.' A score of 15 represents the most jealous person. A score of 0 represents the most secure.

ANSWERS

PRE-TEST

Answers	Page Numbers
1. C	160
2. B	180
3. A	165
4. A	171
5. C	166
6. C	162
7. A	169
8. A	159
9. B	161
10. B	165
11. B	165
12. C	172
13. B	161
14. B	162
15. A	164
16. B	173
17. A	159
18. A	170
19. C	160
20. B	173
21. C	174
22. C	165
23. C	162
24. A	176
25. A	159

KEY TERMS CROSSWORD PUZZLE

Across	Page Numbers
1. Secure	162
4. Storge	165
5. Arousal	159
6. Agape	165
9. Narcissist	172
12. Mania	165
13. Ludus	165
14. Arranged	180

Down	
2. Cyberstalking	174
3. Homophobia	170
7. Pragma	165
8. Avoidant	162
10. Intimacy	160
11. Eros	165
15. Desire	159

POST-TEST

Answers	Page Numbers
1. B	173
2. C	171
3. B	172
4. B	160
5. C	166
6. C	165
7. B	165
8. A	163
9. A	161
10. B	173
11. B	171
12. A	165
13. B	159
14. B	164
15. B	180
16. B	165
17. C	160
18. C	163
19. B	165
20. A	162
21. A	165
22. C	179
23. A	180
24. B	160
25. B	170

SEXUALITY AND SEXUAL EXPRESSION THROUGHOUT LIFE

7

CHAPTER OBJECTIVES

Upon reading Chapter Seven, students should be able to:

1. Discuss the components of sexuality.

2. Explain the reasons why we have sex.

3. Discuss the various sources of sexual information.

4. Describe different sexual behaviors.

5. Discuss how sexuality changes throughout the life course.

6. Compare and contrast pre-marital and marital sex.

7. Explain sexual infidelity.

8. Discuss gay, lesbian, and bisexual sex.

9. Compare and contrast sexually transmitted diseases.

CHAPTER OVERVIEW

Sexuality is the product of sexual identity, sexual orientation, and sexual scripts. *Sexual identity* is an awareness of self as male or female and includes *sexual desire, sexual response,* and *gender roles. Sexual orientation* refers to preference for partners. **Homosexuals** are sexually attracted to people of the same sex and include *gays* (men) and *lesbians* (women). **Heterosexuals** are attracted to partners of the opposite sex and are often called straight. **Bisexuals,** or bis, are attracted to members of both sexes. **Asexuals** lack any interest in or desire to have sex. Although heterosexuality is the predominant sexual orientation, homosexuality exists in all known societies. Many gay men and lesbians deny or try to suppress their sexual preference due to **heterosexism**, the belief that heterosexuality is superior to and more natural than homosexuality. About 2 percent of Americans are *transgendered*, men and women who do not identify with any specific gender category. Transgendered individuals include: *transsexuals* (born one sex but live as opposite sex), *intersexuals* (medical diagnosis at birth not clearly male or female) and *transvestites* (cross-dressers). *Biological theories* suggest that sexual orientation has a genetic base. Cultural theories hold that sexual orientation is the result of social and environmental factors.

There are more similarities between heterosexual and homosexual men than between lesbians and gays. **Sexual scripts**, the norms for sexual activity, are shaped by gender, race, and ethnicity. The *sexual double standard* suggests that sexual intercourse outside of marriage is acceptable for men, but not for women.

The reasons that we have sex the first time include interpersonal matters, peer pressure, parental inputs, and structural factors. Those in short-term committed relationships have sex to express affection, to increase *intimacy* (closeness), to encourage *self-disclosure* (revealing feelings), and to *exchange resources*. Those in long-term committed relationships have sex to maintain relationship, foster *interdependence*, and procreate. Many adolescents and young adults lack knowledge and have serious misconceptions about sex. Our main sources of sexual information include parents, peers, the media, popular culture, and sex education programs in schools.

Autoeroticism, arousal of sexual feelings without an external stimulus, commonly includes sexual fantasies and **masturbation** (sexual self-pleasuring that involves direct physical stimulation). Oral sex, or outercourse, includes **fellatio** (oral stimulation of a man's penis) and **cunnilingus** (oral stimulation of a woman's genitals). *Coitus* refers to penile-vaginal penetration. **Sexual response** is the physiological response to sexual stimulation. Adolescent sex is predicated by peer pressure, parental factors, environmental variables, and cultural attitudes. Abstinence is promoted among Latina teens by *verguenza* (shame) and *marianismo* (expectation of virginity). Girls are the victims of forced sex more than boys. For girls, the most common factors associated with unwanted sex are a mother's with an abusive boyfriend, illicit drug use, lack of monitoring in the home, a history of sexual abuse in the victim's family, and the victim's living apart from parents before coming of age. Males are more likely than females to initiate sexual intercourse. Compared to singles, married couples have sex more often and are happier with their sex lives. However, the frequency of marital sex declines with time.

Menopause is the cessation of the menstrual cycle and the loss of reproductive capacity. It is unclear whether there is a **male climacteric**, or change of life analogous to females, because men do not lose their reproductive capacity. Sexual activity among older people declines, but does not disappear. The double standard persists throughout old age in that men do not face the same pressures as women to look young. The biggest impediment to sex as people age is the partner gap: there is a small pool of available mates.

Emotional infidelity includes *secrecy* (meeting someone without telling your spouse or partner), *emotional intimacy* (confiding things you have not told your spouse), and *sexual chemistry* (being mutually attracted to someone). Extramarital sex is not common. Macro-reasons for extramarital sex include economic problems, the changing purpose of marriage, anonymity in urban life, greater opportunities, increased life expectancy, and new technology. Micro-reasons include emotional satisfaction, loneliness, ego-enhancement, social exchange, revenge, and ending the marriage .

Researchers generally measure the extent of homosexuality by simply asking people how they identify themselves. About 8% of Americans identify themselves as homosexual or bisexual. However, 18% have had same-sex sexual contact. **Homophobia** is the fear and hatred of homosexuality and often takes the form of *gay bashing* (threats, assaults, or acts of violence). More than half of Americans believe that homosexuality is an acceptable way of life.

Sexually transmitted infections (STIs) are diseases that are spread by sexual or nonsexual contact with body parts or fluids that harbor specific microorganisms. The most common STIs are *chlamydia* and *gonorrhea. Human papilloma virus* causes genital warts and may lead to cervical cancer. *HIV* (human immunodeficiency virus) causes *AIDS* (acquired immunodeficiency syndrome), which is a degenerative condition that attacks the body's immune system and renders it unable to fight a number of diseases, including pneumonia and cancer.

PRE-TEST

1. Because Violet did not get treatment for a sexually transmitted infection, she developed Pelvic Inflammatory Disease (PID). The untreated ailment was:
   - a. Chlamydia
   - b. Genital warts
   - c. Gonorrhea

1. Jack and Christy had sex and both experienced an orgasm. This biological aspect of sexuality is called:
    a. Sexual response
    b. Sexual desire
    c. Sexual orientation

2. Mike is a man who prefers sex with other men. This preference refers to Mike's
    a. Sexual orientation
    b. Autoeroticism
    c. Sexual response

3. Flora is set on seducing her man tonight. She engages in oral stimulation of his penis. This is called:
    a. Fellatio
    b. Cunnilingus
    c. Autoeroticism

4. Which of the following is true?
    a. Married people have higher rates of sexual intercourse than singles
    b. Singles have a higher rate of sexual intercourse than married people
    c. There is no difference in the rate of sexual intercourse between married people and singles

5. When Bill Clinton said that he did not have sexual relations with Monica Lewinsky, he was referring to penile-vaginal penetration or:
    a. Fellatio
    b. Coitus
    c. Cunnilingus

6. Candace just found out that she has the sexually transmitted infection that may lead to cervical cancer. Candace has been diagnosed with:
    a. Human immunodeficiency virus (HIV)
    b. Human pappiloma virus (HPV)
    c. Chlamydia

7. Michael and Lisa just had a baby. When they ask the doctor if they had a boy or a girl, the doctor says, "The sex of this baby is unclear." Michael and Lisa's baby is:
    a. Asexual
    b. A transvestite
    c. Intersexual

8. Jane is diagnosed with the most common sexually transmitted infection. Jane has:
   a. Syphilis
   b. Chlamydia
   c. Human pappiloma virus

9. In Nigeria, laws prescribe 14 years of imprisonment for homosexuality because it is believed that heterosexuality is natural and homosexuality is unnatural. This belief refers to:
   a. Homophobia
   b. Heterosexism
   c. Autoeroticism

10. Ed is a man who likes to dress up in women's clothing. As a cross-dresser, Ed is a/an:
    a. Intersexual
    b. Transvestite
    c. Asexual

11. Phyllis is a lesbian. Phyllis believes that her preference for other women is genetic. This supports:
    a. Biological theories
    b. Cultural theories
    c. Both a & b

12. Stephanie and Kevin are a married couple. They are experiencing economic problems. According to the chapter, these problems increase the risk of:
    a. Divorce
    b. Extramarital sex
    c. Masturbation

13. Geraldine watches a movie which portrays a fear and hatred of homosexuals. The movie depicts:
    a. Homophobia
    b. Endorphins
    c. Narcissism

14. Mrs. Chancellor recently went through the change of life. As such, she has experienced the cessation of the menstrual cycle and the loss of reproductive capacity. This is known as:
    a. Climacteric
    b. Fellatio
    c. Menopause

15. The year is 1999 and Eileen and Debbie are a lesbian couple. They have decided to move to the state in which the Supreme Court ruled that same sex partners should have the same rights as married couples. The couple is moving to:
    a. Utah
    b. California
    c. Vermont

16. Wendy's classmates physically assaulted her when they found out that she was a lesbian. This reflects:
    a. Gay bashing
    b. Homophobia
    c. Both a & b

17. In the Seaver household, it is acceptable for the sons to have girls alone in their rooms, but the daughters must entertain company in the family room when family is present. This illustrates:
    a. Heterosexism
    b. The sexual double standard
    c. The sexual revolution

18. Mary and Jerry had sex in an effort to foster interdependence. Like most couples who have sex for interdependence, Mary and Jerry are in:
    a. A long-term committed relationship
    b. A short-term committed relationship
    c. None of the above

19. In the Latino community, the norm is for males to be highly sexual. This gives an example of:
    a. Sexual scripts
    b. Hormones
    c. Autoeroticism

20. Ahmad and Alicia are a married couple, but Ahmad does not confide in his wife. Instead, he shares his innermost thoughts and feelings with his colleague, Sharon. This illustrates which component of emotional infidelity?
    a. Sexual chemistry
    b. Secrecy
    c. Emotional intimacy

21.   Lisa has been taking medication for mental illness. As a result, Lisa has no interest in having sex. Lisa is:
    a. Asexual
    b. Homosexual
    c. Heterosexual

22.   Inez is a Latina who believes that good girls should not know about sexuality. In Inez's culture, the 'shame' and embarrassment about body parts is called:
    a.   Marianismo
    b.   Machismo
    c.   Verguenza

23.   Timmy, who is gay, is having a debate with his older brother, Robert about similarities and differences among gays and straights. Which of the following is true?
    a.   There are more similarities in gender roles between lesbians and gays than straight and gay men
    b.   There are more similarities in gender roles between straight and gay men than there are between lesbians and gays
    c.   There are no similarities in the gender roles of gay and straight men

24.   Yoto has sex with his wife Suki about three times a week. Yoto hopes to keep this pace up for the next 75 years. However, research suggests that the frequency of Yoto's sexual activity will begin to decrease significantly at the age of:
    a. 60
    b. 70
    c. 80

APPLICATIONS/EXERCISES

1.   Pretend that you are the parent of a pair of twins, a girl and a boy. They are aged fifteen and they have asked you to talk with them about sex. Having read chapter 7 in the textbook, what would you say to your children? Are there differences in what you would say to the son as opposed to the daughter? How does the double standard impact your conversation?

2.   Recall the reasons that spouses and partners are unfaithful. What societal factors should be changed to reduce the number of people who engage in extramarital affairs? What advice would you give a newly married couple to help prevent infidelity?

CHAPTER 7 KEY TERMS CROSSWORD PUZZLE

Across
2. Oral stimulation of his penis
5. Oral sex
6. Chlamydia is the most common
8. Shame among Latinas
12. Cross-dressers
13. Fear of gays

Down
1. Norms of sexual activity
3. Homosexual women
4. Self pleasure by direct contact
5. Sexual preference
7. Her change of life
9. Homosexual men
10. Oral stimulation of her genitals
11. Lacks sexual desire
13. Leads to AIDS

POST-TEST

1. Mr. & Mrs. Evans are going to talk to their children about sex tonight. They are going to tell their son to use protection if he has sex but they will tell their daughter that she should wait until she is married. This illustrates:
   a. the sexual double standard
   b. the sexual revolution
   c. heterosexism

2. Tracy's baby is blind because at the time of the birth Tracy had:
   a. Chlamydia
   b. Gonorrhea
   c. HIV

3. Jason is attracted to both males and females. As such, Jason is:
   a. Homosexual
   b. Heterosexual
   c. Bisexual

4. The Nixons have a son and a daughter, and both children masturbate. Mrs. Nixon wonders who masturbates more. Research suggests:
   a. Males masturbate more frequently than females
   b. Females masturbate more frequently than males
   c. Males and females are equally likely to masturbate

5. Richard wants both his son and daughter to actively avoid becoming infected with HIV. He spends an equal amount of time with both of them to emphasize this. Richard should know that:
   a. Males are more vulnerable to HIV than females
   b. Females are more vulnerable to HIV than males
   c. Males and females are equally vulnerable to HIV

6. Barbara is a female who prefers to have sex with other women. This preference refers to Barbara's:
   a. Sexual orientation
   b. Autoeroticism
   c. Sexual response

7. Tanya believes that most people cheat. Lori believes that most people do not. Which of the following is true?
   a. Most married Americans have been faithful.
   b. Most married Americans have not been faithful.
   c. There is no difference is the number of married people who are faithful and the number of married people who cheat.

8. In Egypt, gays can be stoned, imprisoned, or killed because it is believed that homosexuality is unnatural and heterosexuality is natural. This belief reflects:
   a. heterosexism
   b. homophobia
   c. autoeroticism

9. Jamie is a hermaphrodite. She was born with both male and female genitals. As such, Jamie is:
   a. A transvestite
   b. Asexual
   c. Intersexual

10. Lloyd often arouses himself by masturbation. This self-pleasuring is an example of:
    a. Heterosexism
    b. Autoeroticism
    c. Homosexuality

11. Which of the following is true?
    a. Married couples are more satisfied with their sex life than singles
    b. Singles are more satisfied with their sex life than married couples
    c. There is no difference in sexual satisfaction between the married and singles

12. When Jada walks into the room with her sexy lingerie, her husband Will gets an erection. This physiological response to sexual stimulation is called:
    a. Sexual desire
    b. Sexual response
    c. Autoeroticism

13. Tawanda has just been diagnosed with the degenerative condition that attacks the body's immune system and renders it unable to fight a number of diseases. Tawanda has:
    a. AIDS
    b. Chlamydia
    c. Syphilis

14. Wesley was assaulted after work when some customers learned that he was gay. This hate crime illustrates:
    a. Homophobia
    b. Gay bashing
    c. Both a & b

15. Which of the following is true?
    a. Most Americans believe that homosexuality is an acceptable way of life
    b. Most Americans believe that homosexuality is not an acceptable way of life
    c. Research has not been conducted to determine how Americans feel about homosexuality

16. Joseph helped his wife reach an orgasm by orally stimulating her genitals. This is an example of:
    a. Fellatio
    b. Cunnilingus
    c. Autoeroticism

17. Ramon and his wife Lolita are in their early seventies. People say that Ramon looks distinguished, but that Lolita is an old bag. This difference refers to:
    a. The double standard
    b. The sexual standard
    c. Climacteric

18. Billy is a gay man. He says that he grew up in a house as the only boy with eight sisters and no male role model. As a result, Billy suggests that he always wanted to be a female and that he always liked boys. This supports:
    a. Biological theories
    b. Sociological theories
    c. Both a & b

19. The year is 1999 and Jarrod and Bruce are a gay couple. They have faced a lot of discrimination and they would like to move to a place where they will be accepted. They move to the state in which the Supreme Court ruled that same sex partners should have the same rights as married couples. The couple moved to:
    a. Utah
    b. California
    c. Vermont

20. Donna has noticed an attitudinal difference in her 55 year old husband. She wonders if he is going through a change similar to menopause. Donna thinks he may be experiencing:
    a. Male climacteric
    b. Autoeroticism
    c. Cunnilingus

21. Before Marty learned that his eldest son was gay, he had a fear and hatred of homosexuals. Back then, Marty was:
    a. Narcissistic
    b. Homophobic
    c. Jealous

22. In Nosha's mind, the male is always supposed to initiate sexual activities. This norm which guides her behavior is also called a:
    a. Sexual script
    b. Sexual identity
    c. Sexual script

23. Don is a man who likes to dress up in women's clothes. Don is a/an:
    a. Homosexual
    b. Intersexual
    c. Transvestite

24. Thurmond belongs to the age group that has the most cases of sexually transmitted infections. Thurmond is:
    a. Under 25
    b. Between 26 and 44
    c. 45 or above

25. Sonia finds sex to be quite pleasurable. The biological response that allows her to enjoy sex is called:
    a. Sexual desire
    b. Sexual response
    c. Sexual orientation

SELF-ASSESSMENT:
HOW CONSERVATIVE IS YOUR SEXUAL SCRIPT?

Directions: Read each statement. Put a check in the box to reflect whether or not you agree.

	Agree	Disagree
Both men and women should initiate sex.		
Masturbation is acceptable.		
Pornography is a significant part of a healthy sex life.		
Casual sex is okay.		
Extramarital sex is acceptable.		
Pre-marital sex is okay.		
Oral sex is acceptable.		
Homosexual relations are acceptable.		
As long as adults are consenting, anything goes.		
Sex is equally pleasing for men and women.		
Sex on the first date is okay.		
Cyber-sex is acceptable.		
A good sex life involves sex in different places.		
Sex involving more than two people is okay.		
Anal sex is acceptable.		
Couples should try different positions when they have sex.		
Digital sex (fingering) is acceptable.		
Kissing should involve various parts of the body.		
It is important to tell a sexual partner what one likes.		
It is okay to have more than one sexual partner.		

Key: Give yourself 1 point for every statement that you checked as 'Agree.' A score of 20 represents the most liberal sexual script. A score of 0 represents the most conservative sexual script.

ANSWERS

PRE-TEST

Answers	Page Numbers
1. C	227
2. A	204
3. A	187
4. A	203
5. A	203
6. B	203
7. B	217
8. C	187
9. B	216
10. B	187
11. B	187
12. A	189
13. B	213
14. A	215
15. C	209
16. C	215
17. C	215
18. B	190
19. A	194
20. A	190
21. C	211
22. A	187
23. C	207
24. A	189
25. B	210

KEY TERMS CROSSWORD PUZZLE

Across	Page Numbers
2. Fellatio	203
5. Outercourse	203
6. STI	216
8. Vergueza	207
12. Transsexuals	187
13. Homophobia	215

Down	
1. Scripts	190
3. Lesbians	187
4. Masturbation	202
5. Orientation	187
7. Menopause	209
9. Gays	187
10. Cunnilingus	203
11. Asexual	187
13. HIV	217

POST-TEST

Answers		Page Numbers
1. A		190
2. B		217
3. C		187
4. A		202
5. B		219
6. A		187
7. A		212
8. A		187
9. C		187
10.	B	201
11.	A	203
12.	B	204
13.	A	217
14.	C	214
15.	A	215
16.	B	203
17.	A	190
18.	B	189
19.	C	215
20.	A	209
21.	B	215
22.	A	190
23.	C	187
24.	A	216
25.	B	204

8

CHOOSING OTHERS: DATING AND MATE SELECTION

CHAPTER OBJECTIVES

Upon reading Chapter Eight students should be able to:

1. Describe the dating process.

2. Explain the functions of dating.

3. Compare and contrast traditional, contemporary, and traditional-contemporary forms of dating.

4. Describe the different methods used by American adults to meet potential mates.

5. Describe the choices and constraints of mate selection.

6. Explain the three theories of mate selection.

7. Discuss cross-cultural differences in mate selection.

8. Discuss power and control in dating relationships.

9. Discuss aggression and violence in dating relationships.

10. Describe how and why couples break up.

CHAPTER OVERVIEW

Dating, the process of meeting people socially for possible mate selection, has been described as a marriage market. A **marriage market** involves prospective spouses comparing the assets and liabilities of eligible partners to choose the best available mate. Dating serves both *manifest* (recognized and intended) and *latent* (unrecognized and unintended) functions. Manifest functions include maturation, recreation, companionship, love, and mate selection. Latent functions include socialization, social status, fulfillment of ego needs, sexual experimentation, and support of the economic market. In *traditional* *dating*, which was common until the 1970s, clearly defined gender roles were followed. Traditional dating is typical in formal events like *coming-out parties* (young women are introduced to society at debutante balls), the *bat mitzvah* (rite of passage for Jewish girls), the *bar mitzvah* (rite of passage for Jewish boys), and the *quinceanera* (celebrates a 15 year old Latina's entrance into adulthood). Traditionally, after a few dates couples would commit to *going steady*, meaning that partners would only see each other. Contemporary dating may be casual or serious. Casual dating includes *hanging out* (setting a meeting place and time where different people come and go), *getting together* (friends meet at someone's house, club, or party), *pack dating* (socializing in unpartnered groups), and *hooking up* (physical encounters with no strings attached). Serious dating, on the other hand, is more likely to lead to cohabitation, engagement, and marriage. Traditional-contemporary combinations of dating include proms, homecoming parties, and dinner dates in which the couples are *going Dutch*, or splitting the costs of a date.

Methods used by adults to meet potential spouses include personal classified ads, mail-order brides, professional matchmakers, speed dating, and cyberdating. With classified ads, females describe themselves as sex objects, and men describe themselves as success objects. Mail-order brides are usually from economically disadvantaged regions in Eastern Europe and South Asia. Beginning in 2006, the international Marriage Broker Regulation Act requires U.S. men seeking a visa for a prospective bride to disclose any criminal convictions for domestic violence, sexual assault, or child abuse. *Speed dating* allows people to meet each other face to face, within a short period of time, to decide if there is a mutual interest in meeting again. *Cyberdating* involves using the internet to find romance.

Filter theory suggests that we sift eligible people according to specific criteria and narrow the pool of potential partners to a small number of candidates. The major filtering mechanism is **homogamy** (dating or marrying someone that is similar). Some of the most important filtering variables are **propinquity** (geographic closeness), physical appearance, race, ethnicity, religion, age, social class, and values. Physically attractive people benefit from the 'halo effect', which assumes that they have other desirable social characteristic. Often used interchangeably with the term exogamy is heterogamy, which is dating someone from a social, racial, ethnic, religious, or age group that is different from one's own. *Interdating* involves going out with a member of a different ethnic or racial group. **Heterogamy** is dating someone from a group that is different from one's own. **Hypergamy** involves marrying up in terms of social class and **hypogamy** involves marrying down. *Social exchange theory* suggests people will begin and remain in a relationship if the rewards are high and the costs are low. **Equity theory**, an extension of social exchange theory, suggests that a relationship is satisfying and stable if both people see it as equitable and mutually beneficial.

Most countries do not have "open" courtship systems. In some societies, the **dowry** (the money, goods, or property a woman brings to a marriage) is an important basis for mate selection. In other cases there is a *bride price*, a required payment by the groom's family. Compared to free choice marriages, in arranged marriages the family and community are more important than the individual.

Major problems in relationships include power, control, and sexual aggression. The *principle of least interest* suggests that the person with more power is less dependent and less interested in maintaining the relationship. Men are more likely than women to use physical force and sexual aggression in dating relationships. Dating violence is rarely a one time event. Women are more vulnerable than men to **acquaintance rape** (victim knows or is familiar with the rapist) and **date rape** (unwanted, forced sexual intercourse in the context of a dating situation). Dating violence and rape may be explained by family violence, *misogyny* (hatred of women), peer pressure, secrecy, and alcohol and drugs.

There are individual and structural reasons for ending relationships. Responses to break-ups up vary. Those who have a high value on the marriage market are less upset by break-ups than those who have a lower value. Knowing the reason for the break-up provides a sense of closure. Men seem to get over breakups more quickly than women. Although painful, breaking up is a normal step in the process of dating and filtering out unsuitable mates. Ending a relationship provides a chance to find a more suitable mate. Yet, breaking up a marriage is more complicated than dating or cohabiting relationships.

PRE-TEST

1. Barry is a stockbroker. He believes that dating is similar to buying stocks in that you compare the assets and liabilities of eligible partners and choose the best available mate. Barry sees dating as:
   a. Propinquity
   b. A marriage market
   c. A dowry

2. Enrique is dating for fun and recreation. This illustrates a _____, or intended, function of dating.
   a. Manifest
   b. Latent
   c. Both a & b

3. It is her 15th birthday, and Elsa's family will celebrate her entrance into adulthood with a:
   a. Bar mitzvah
   b. Bat mitzvah
   c. Quinceanera

4. Grandmother likes to tell the story of how she and Grandfather met, fell in love, and married. She says that they spent seven months going steady. This means that for seven months, they were:
   a. Engaged
   b. Only seeing one another
   c. Group dating

5. When Niesa and Amadou married, her family provided them with $5,000, 10 acres of land, and a herd of cattle. The money, goods, and property make up the:
   a. Bride price
   b. Dowry
   c. Propinquity

6. In the movie "Pretty Woman," the upper class businessman married the lower class prostitute. In marrying a prostitute, the man married down. This is called:
   a. Hypergamy
   b. Homogamy
   c. Hypogamy

7. Leroy and Keisha are going out on a date for the very first time. They have agreed to split the costs of the dinner and the movie. This is called:
   a. Going steady
   b. Going Dutch
   c. Going together

8. Max is looking for a mate and has decided to place an ad in the classified section of the local newspaper. Like most men placing ads, Max will describe himself as:
   a. Successful
   b. Sexy
   c. Beautiful and sexy

9. Leinu hopes to be a mail-order bride for an American man, but her mother is concerned about Leinu's safety. Leinu tells her mother, "Don't worry, because of _____, we would know if the man has a history of violence."
   a. International Mail Order Bride Act
   b. International Marriage Broker Regulation Act
   c. International Disclosure of Criminal Convictions Act

10. The school is hosting a "Turnabout" prom in which the women will extend invitations to the prom. This is an example of:
   a. Contemporary dating
   b. Traditional dating
   c. Traditional-contemporary dating

11. Willis and Charlene have been together for four months. They met online at matchmaker.com. This is an example of:
   a. Interdating
   b. Cyberdating
   c. Speed dating

12. Rafeal is intimidated because his wife Rosa makes more money than he does. Rafael believes that men should make more money than their wives. As such, Rafael believes that:
   a. Men should be hypogamous
   b. Women should be hypogamous
   c. Both a & b

13. Lynnetta and Brutus are on their first date and she asks him 20 questions to see if he fits her criteria. He does not fit her criteria and when he asks if she wants to go out again, she declines. Which theory best explains Lynetta's sifting?
   a. Social exchange theory
   b. Filter theory
   c. Equity theory

14. Shante is a 24 year-old African American woman and is dating a 24 year-old African American man. As Shante is dating someone with similar social characteristics, this is an example of:
   a. Homogamy
   b. Heterogamy
   c. Hypergamy

15. Katie says that she would never do a long distance relationship. She wants a man who lives in her town. Katie is concerned about geographic closeness or:
    a. Propinquity
    b. Dowry
    c. Misogyny

16. Gwen attended an event organized at the student union where the participants went from one table to another spending 5 minutes chatting with each person. At the end of the event she decided which people she would like to see again. This is an example of:
    a. Cyberdating
    b. Speed dating
    c. Interdating

17. Reggie lists the rewards and costs of staying with his girlfriend. Reggie examines his list and notices that he is getting just as much as he is giving. Which theory suggests that Reggie will continue the relationship?
    a. Filter Theory
    b. Equity Theory
    c. Social Exchange Theory

18. Tanya and her boyfriend Edward are being forced by their parents to break up. Based on research on gender differences and break up, who will probably get over the relationship quicker?
    a. Tanya
    b. Edward
    c. There is no research on gender differences in break ups.

19. Hadassa is Jewish and her husband is Catholic. Because the two belong to different social groups, this illustrates:
    a. Hypogamy
    b. Heterogamy
    c. Homogamy

20. When Sambath and Oka married, the groom's family paid the bride's family $1,500. This payment is an example of:
    a. Equity
    b. Dowry
    c. Bride price

21. Tony and Angela are a married couple. Angela is considering divorce, but Tony wants to try to work out their problems and maintain the relationship. The principle of least interest suggests that:
   a. Tony has more power
   b. Angela has more power
   c. The power is equally shared

22. The tapes from the hidden video camera reveal that after sedating his patients, Dr. Dyce sexually assaulted them. This is an example of:
   a. Date rape
   b. Acquaintance rape
   c. Both a & b

23. Marcia is a rape victim. She believes that the man who raped her did so because of a hatred of women. The hatred of women is called:
   a. Misogyny
   b. Dowry
   c. Propinquity

24. Ross and Phoebe are debating about whether men or women snoop into their partners things more often. The research suggests that:
   a. Men are more likely than women to keep tabs on a partner
   b. Women are more likely than men to keep tabs on a partner
   c. Men and women are equally likely to keep tabs on a partner

25. At a recent fraternity party, some young men slipped a drug into Tina's dink and raped her. The date rape drug may have been:
   a. Rohypnol
   b. GHB
   c. Both a & b

EXERCISES/APPLICATIONS

1.   Filter theory suggests that we limit our pool of eligibles using set criteria. If you were to create a filter for selecting your ideal mate, what criteria would you use? How does homogamy and heterogamy impact your filter?

2.   There are numerous methods used by American adults looking for a mate. These include personal ads, mail-order brides, cyberdating, and speed dating. Would you feel comfortable telling friends and family about how you met your spouse through one of these methods? Why or why not?

CHAPTER 8 KEY TERMS CROSSWORD PUZZLE

Across

3. When he's Black & she's White
5. Victim knows rapist
8. Spouse is different
9. Unrecognized and unintended
10. Bride takes it to the marriage
11. Picking her up in a chat-room
12. Marry up

Down

1. Groom's family pays
2. Geographic closeness
4. Theory that extends exchange theory
6. Spouse is like you
7. Recognized and intended
8. Marry down

POST-TEST

1. While babysitting, Teresa was sexually assaulted by her client. This illustrates:
   a. Date rape
   b. Acquaintance rape
   c. Both a & b

2. The students have complained about Dr. Knowitall for years. He constantly bashes women in his classes. It is commonly believed that he hates women, which would be:
   a. Propinquity
   b. Dowry
   c. Misogyny

3. Marlon and Regina are dating, and Regina wants the relationship much more than Marlon. The principle of least interest suggests that:
   a. Marlon has the most power
   b. Regina has the most power
   c. The power is equally shared

4. Naomi says, "In my marriage I give, give, give, and my husband Vinton just takes, takes, takes!" Which theory suggests that this marriage will end?
   a. Conflict theory
   b. Equity theory
   c. Filter theory

5. Paul lives in California and Sara lives in New York. The two have had a long distance relationship for the last 7 years. To them, geographic closeness, or _____, does not matter
   a. Equity
   b. Propinquity
   c. Dowry

6. Hector and Beatriz are dating. They are both Mexican American. Because they belong to the same social group, this illustrates:
   a. Heterogany
   b. Hypogamy
   c. Homogamy

7. There are six women that are interested in Martin. To narrow down this pool, Martin uses age as his criterion. He wants a young woman, so he rejects the oldest women. Which theory best explains Martin's use of age to sift out the best mate?
   a. Filter theory
   b. Equity theory
   c. Social exchange theory

8. Myra just started an online dating service to help match single mothers with single fathers. Myra's website revolves around:
   a. Interdating
   b. Cyberdating
   c. Speed dating

9. Hannah is a student in a marriage and family class. During class, she asks Professor Riddle his age. Seeing an opportunity to get Hannah involved in research, the professor tells her that he is a part of the fastest-growing group of online dating service users. Professor Riddle is:
   a. Between 25 and 39
   b. Between 40 and 54
   c. 55 or older

10. After being released from prison for sexual assault, Chad is fed up with American women and their independence and decides to get a mail-order bride. However, Chad is prevented from doing so because of his criminal conviction. Which law stopped Chad?
   a. International Mail Order Bride Act
   b. International Marriage Broker Regulation Act
   c. International Disclosure of Criminal Convictions Act

11. Cynthia is looking for a mate and has decided to place an ad in the classified section of the local newspaper. Like most women placing an ad, Cynthia will describe herself as:
   a. Ambitious
   b. Beautiful
   c. Educated

12. The debutante ball is a coming-out party where thirty upper class young women accompanied by male escorts will be introduced to society. This is an example of:
   a. Traditional dating
   b. Contemporary dating
   c. Traditional-contemporary dating

13. Borat's car broke down and he has to pay to get it fixed. Because he is short on cash, he asks Anissa if she will pay for half of the expenses from the date. He is asking her to:
    a. Go Dutch
    b. Go steady
    c. Go together

14. In the classic story of Cinderella, a poor girl marries a rich prince. The poor girl married up the social ladder. This illustrates:
    a. Hypogamy
    b. Hypergamy
    c. Homogamy

15. A group of teenagers met at the Smith household for some no-strings attached oral sex. In contemporary dating terms this is called:
    a. An orgy
    b. Pack dating
    c. Hooking up

16. For years Mr. Roth has promised his son Josh that he will be able to date once he passes through the cultural rite of passage for Jewish boys known as the:
    a. Bar mitzvah
    b. Bat mitzvah
    c. Quinceanera

17. Serigne and Liala are getting married. The groom's family gives the bride's family $10,000. This is an example of:
    a. Propinquity
    b. Bride price
    c. Dowry

18. Michelle is dating James in an effort to enhance her own status. After all, girls who have a boyfriend are more popular than girls who do not. This illustrates the _____, or unintended, function of dating.
    a. Latent
    b. Manifest
    c. Both a & b

19. Clarissa wants a man. She is currently dating several different men, comparing their assets and liabilities so that she can choose the one that is best. This illustrates:
    a. A marriage market
    b. A dowry
    c. A bride price

20. Anna Nicole is nineteen years old and she marries a man that is her grandfather's age. Because the two belong to different social groups, this illustrates:
    a. Heterogamy
    b. Homogamy
    c. Hypogamy

21. Jarrod has spent a total of $400 on 8 dates and is still alone. His friends tell him that for $30 he can meet 8 people at an event where each participant goes from table to table spending 5 minutes chatting with a different person to determine if there is any chemistry. Jarrod say that he will give this event, called _____, a chance.
    a. Speed dating
    b. Cyberdating
    c. Interdating

22. Victor follows traditional gender role scripts. As such, Victor believes that:
    a. Men should be hypogamous
    b. Women should be hypogamous
    c. Both a & b

23. Tunga and Lergo are marrying. The bride's family gives the married couple a flock of sheep. This is an example of:
    a. Bride price
    b. Dowry
    c. Propinquity

24. The Barone family owns a floral shop near campus. Most of their clients are college students in dating relations. The economic profits that the Barones receive from flower sales illustrate the _____ function of dating.
    a. Latent
    b. Manifest
    c. Both a & b

25. Victoria and Cole have a relationship that is perceived to be mutually beneficial. Which theory suggests that their relationship is stable and satisfying?
    a. Conflict theory
    b. Equity theory
    c. Filter theory

SELF-ASSESSMENT:
HOW HEALTHY ARE YOUR BREAK UPS?

Directions: Read each statement. Put a check in the box to reflect whether or not you agree.

	Agree	Disagree
If a couple breaks up, they are not meant to be together.		
Break ups are a normal part of life.		
I can forgive a person for the hurt caused by a break-up.		
I have a lot to offer a potential mate.		
A break-up should be done in person.		
If someone I loved tried to leave me, I would try to convince them to stay.		
People can truly love more than one person in a lifetime.		
Breaking up can be a good thing.		
After a break-up, I lean on my friends for support.		
Break-ups provide opportunities for personal growth.		
After a break-up, I can still say nice things about an ex.		
I handle break-ups with maturity.		
If someone broke up with me, I would want to know why.		
Breaking up involves a period of mourning the loss.		
After a break-up, I recover quickly.		

Key: Give yourself 1 point for every statement that you checked as 'Agree.' A score of 15 represents the healthiest attitudes toward break-ups. A score of 0 represents the least healthy and suggests much room for improvement.

ANSWERS

POST-TEST

Answers	Page Numbers
1. B	250
2. C	251
3. A	248
4. B	242
5. B	235
6. C	235
7. A	234
8. B	233
9. C	233
10. B	252
11. B	231
12. A	227
13. A	238
14. B	240
15. C	228
16. A	227
17. B	244
18. A	226
19. A	225
20. A	240
21. A	232
22. A	240
23. B	244
24. A	226
25. B	242

SINGLEHOOD, COHABITATION, CIVIL UNIONS & OTHER OPTIONS

9

CHAPTER OBJECTIVES

Upon reading Chapter Nine, students should be able to:

1.   Explain recent trends in singlehood and the demographics of singles in America.

2.   Compare and contrast the four types of single adults.

3.   Explain the macro and micro factors that impact singlehood.

4.   Discuss recent trends in cohabitation and the demographics of cohabitors

5.   Compare and contrast the various types of cohabitation

6.   Compare and contrast the benefits and costs of cohabitation.

7.   Discuss cohabitation among gays and lesbians.

8.   Describe patterns of communal living.

CHAPTER OVERVIEW

The single population is growing. There are four types of singles: *voluntary temporary* (open to marriage, but it is a low priority), *voluntary stable* (has no interest in marrying or remarrying), involuntary temporary (would like marry and is actively seeking mates), and *involuntary stable* (wanted to marry or remarry, but did not, and now accepts single status). For older singles, the double standard favors men. Women, whites, and older adults are more likely to live alone. Macro-level factors that affect singles include war, technology, social movements, economic factors, and gender roles. Demographic shifts include the **sex ratio** (the proportion of men to women in a county), the **marriage squeeze** (a sex imbalance in the ratio of available unmarried women and men), social class, residence, and single parenthood. Individual reasons for being single include ideas about soul mates, being independent, close relationships, commitment, children, fear of divorce, and attractiveness. There are racial and ethnic differences among singles. Blacks are most likely to be single. Among Latinos, *familism* encourages marriage and having children. Asian Americans and Pacific Islanders have some of the lowest rates of singlehood.

Cohabitation, a living arrangement in which two people who are not related and not married live together and usually have a sexual relationship, is on the rise. The U.S. Census Bureau calls cohabitants **POSSLQs**, persons of the opposite sex sharing living quarters. Most cohabiting relationships are short lived. There are several types of cohabitation: **serial cohabitation** (living with one partner for a time and then with another), **dating cohabitation** (couple spends a great deal of time together and eventually decides to move in together), **premarital cohabitation** (couple is testing the relationship before making a final commitment), **trial marriage** (partners want to see what marriage might be like), **substitute marriage** (a long-term commitment between two people without a legal marriage). Like other lifestyles, cohabitation has advantages and disadvantages. Divorce rates are higher for those who cohabit than people who do not live together before marriage. There are three explanations for this trend: *the selection effect* (cohabitors are poor marriage risks), *the cohabitation experience effect* (cohabitors think of relationships as temporary), and the *inertia effect* (cohabitors drift into marriage). Children of cohabitors fare worse than children of married couples in that they: experience more domestic violence; are more likely to be poor; live in households where more money is spent on adult-oriented goods; and have more academic, emotional, and behavioral problems. Cohabitants and their children have little legal protection in the U.S. As cohabitation becomes more prevalent globally, many countries have extended cohabitants the same rights as married couples.

Because legal marriage is rare for homosexuals, many turn to cohabitation. Some newspapers in the U.S. run same-sex commitment notices, allowing gays and lesbians to publicly proclaim their love and commitment. The majority of homosexual couples have equal power in their relationships. Gay life is not divided into butch and femme. Specialization in masculine and feminine activities is typically based on individual skills and interests. Like heterosexual couples, gay and lesbian couples experience conflict in four areas: *power, personal flaws, intimacy,* and *physical absence.* Nevertheless, violence is more prevalent among gay couples than either lesbian or heterosexual cohabitants. Gay and lesbian couples tend to get less social support from family members than heterosexual couples. The 1996 Defense of Marriage Act bans federal benefits for same sex spouses and holds that no state is required to respect a marriage between homosexuals. Same sex couples can enter into *civil unions*, which provide some entitlements to the legal benefits of marriage. Vermont was the first state to recognize such unions. In 2004, Massachusetts was the fist stat to legalize same-sex marriage. Several countries have legalized same-sex marriages.

Communes are collective households in which children and adults from different families live together. Communal living is common on many college campuses among fraternities and sororities. A new program, Co-Abode, matches low income single mothers in subsidized housing. A growing number of elderly people also choose communal living rather than moving in with children or living in nursing homes. Communal alternatives for the elderly include: *retirement communities* (apartments for residents who are self-sufficient), *homesharing* (two or more people sharing a home or apartment), *elderly cottage housing opportunities* (small portables that can be placed beside single-family housing), *continuing care retirement communities* (allows residents to access the housing options and services needed), *assisted living facilities* (provides housing, meals, personal care, social activities and minimal nursing care), and *board and care homes* (provides a room, meals, and help with daily activities).

PRE-TEST

1. The year is 2003. Chester is an unmarried 26 year old man. His grandparents think that it is very strange that Chester is still single. His grandparents should know that:
   a. Half of all American men are older than Chester when they marry for the first time
   b. Half of all men are younger than Chester when they marry for the first time
   c. Half of all men are Chester's age when they marry for the first time

2. Javier is a college student. He will marry one day. But right now, his main priorities include finishing school, establishing his career, and buying his own home. Javier is which type of single?
   a. Voluntary temporary
   b. Voluntary stable
   c. Involuntary temporary

3. Joseph moved in with Myra for 7 months and then left her and moved in with Thomasina for 16 months. Now, he is moving in with Rita. This illustrates:
   a. Polygamous cohabitation
   b. Substitute marriage
   c. Serial cohabitation

4. Hilda's first husband was physically and emotionally abusive. Once Hilda escaped that bad situation through a nasty divorce, she decided that she would never marry again. Hilda is content with being single. As such, Hilda is which type of single?
   a. Involuntary stable
   b. Voluntary stable
   c. Voluntary temporary

5. James and Michelle have been dating for 15 months and they are not yet sure if they would like to marry one another. They move in together to test their relationship before making a final commitment. This illustrates:
   a. Premarital cohabitation
   b. Trial marriage
   c. Substitute marriage

6. Marcia and Greg would like to get married but Marcia is underage and needs her mother's permission. Her mother will not sign the permission slip because she believes that Marcia and Greg are too young. The couple will have to wait until they are older to get married. Marcia and Greg are which type of singles?
   a. Voluntary temporary
   b. Involuntary stable
   c. Involuntary temporary

7. Mike and Doreen lived together for 9 months before getting married. Even though they married, they continued to view their relationship as temporary. Both felt if it did not work out, they would just leave. After 18 months, they divorced. This is explained by the:
   a. Cohabitation experience effect
   b. Selection effect
   c. Inertia effect

8. Lenny and Sylvia have been living together for 22 years. Lenny is unable to marry Sylvia because he is still legally married to another woman. This arrangement illustrates:
   a. Trial marriage
   b. Serial cohabitation
   c. Substitute marriage

9. Horatio has a terminal illness. The doctors have given him 3 months to live. Although Horatio always wanted to settle down and get married, now he realizes that he will die a single man. Horatio is which type of single?
   a. Involuntary stable
   b. Involuntary temporary
   c. Voluntary temporary

10. Lillian and Leslie are a lesbian couple who live together. Although Lillian works for the federal government, her partner is not eligible to receive the federal benefits that married heterosexual couples are entitled to. This is because of the 1996:
    a. Defense of Marriage Act
    b. Family Benefits Coverage Act
    c. Cohabitation Exclusionary Act

11. Swahila is researching communes. She learns that the communal program, Co-abode, matches _____ in subsidized housing.
    a. First time in college students
    b. Elderly people that are self-sufficient
    c. Low-income single mothers

12. Ramon and his wife Lolita are in their early seventies. People say that Ramon looks "distinguished" but that Lolita is an "old bag." This difference refers to:
    a. The double standard
    b. The sexual standard
    c. Climacteric

13. The Maxwell twins, a male and a female, have just graduated from college. Which one is more likely to live alone
    a. The son
    b. The daughter
    c. They are equally likely

14. Lonnie is a 38 year old woman, and although she would like to get married and have a baby, she is in no rush because many women in their 40s and 50s are having healthy babies. Lonnie is not pressured by her biological clock because of changes in:
    a. Gender roles
    b. The marriage squeeze
    c. Technology

15. Nathaniel and Henry are a gay couple. Terrell and Sherry are a heterosexual couple. Which couple is more likely to have an egalitarian relationship?
    a. Nathaniel and Henry
    b. Terrell and Sherry
    c. They are equally likely

16. In North Africa, the sex ratio is 94. This means that there are:
    a. 94 men for every 100 women
    b. 94 women for every 100 men
    c. Equal numbers of men and women.

17. Charlotte and Milo are engaged to be married. Their wedding is scheduled for September but the leases on their apartments were up in June. The two are currently living together as they prepare for the wedding in an effort to save money. This exemplifies:
    a. Trial marriage
    b. Substitute marriage
    c. Premarital cohabitation

18. Jaquetta is a 47 year old female. She desires a husband, but most of the men in her age group desire a woman who is younger than Jaquetta. This means that there are fewer men for Jaquetta to choose from and illustrates the:
    a. Sex ratio
    b. Marriage squeeze
    c. Age standard

19. Thelma is lower class. Penny is middle class. Based on research, who is more likely to find a mate?
    a. Thelma
    b. Penny
    c. They are equally likely

20. Angelo and Donna are an unmarried couple. They just found out that Donna is pregnant. What message is this couple most likely to receive from American society?
    a. It is very important for you to marry
    b. It is not very important for you to marry
    c. None of the above

21. Jennifer has to do a paper on singles and ethnicity. She finds that the lowest rate of singlehood is among:
    a. African Americans
    b. Latinos
    c. Asian Americans

22. "POSSLQ's" is a term used by the U.S. Census Bureau to refer to cohabitants. Who is included in this term?
   a. Heterosexual couples
   b. Homosexual couples
   c. Both a & b

23. Wanda and April are a lesbian couple. They live in the United States, and they would like to publicly proclaim their love and commitment for one another. Which of the following are they most likely to do:
   a. Legally marry
   b. Put a commitment notice in the newspaper
   c. Both a & b

24. Priscilla has done the research on cohabitation and is trying to convince her parents that her decision to move in with her boyfriend is a good one. In support of the research, Priscilla tells them:
   a. Most cohabiting relationships are long-term
   b. She can enjoy companionship while maintaining independence
   c. Both a & b

25. Tomorrow, Jorge must give an in-class presentation on social class and cohabitation. Jorge will report that:
   a. Lower class people are most likely to cohabit
   b. Middle class people are most likely to cohabit
   c. Upper class people are most likely to cohabit

APPLICATIONS/EXERCISES

1. There is a marriage squeeze in America. Consider your local area. Discuss whether or not there is a marriage squeeze. Which groups are most affected and why?

2. There are five myths about singles in America. Think about your favorite television shows that portray the single life style. Which myths about single people are depicted on the shows? How have such portrayals shaped your thoughts about singles?

CHAPTER 9 KEY TERMS CROSSWORD PUZZLE

Across

6. Shacking up
8. Defense of _____ Act
10. 1st state to recognize civil unions
11. Proportion of men to women

Down

1. Almost married
2. Repeated cohabitation
3. Cohabitation for the engaged
4. Potential partner imbalance
5. Collective households
6. Domestic partnerships
7. Caused by drifting into marriage
9. Nickname at the U.S. Census Bureau

POST-TEST

1. Elsa and Imani are a lesbian couple. Jacob and Ross are a gay couple. Which couple is more likely to use violence in their relationship?
   a. Elsa and Imani
   b. Jacob and Ross
   c. They are equally likely

2. Kamili and Nadia have been living together for two years. They have one child, and they split all the financial obligations. The two decide that they may as well get married because they already have the responsibility of a married couple. They divorce after 3 years of marriage. This is explained by the:
   a. Selection effect
   b. Inertia effect
   c. Cohabitation experience effect

3. Mary and Frank are dating. They both consider marriage to be a serious commitment but they are not sure that they have what it takes to make it work. The two are not sure that they want to marry one another, so they move in together to see what marriage might be like. Which type of cohabitation is illustrated?
   a. Premarital cohabitation
   b. Substitute marriage
   c. Trial marriage

4. Saul and Liz are considering moving in together before they get married. They do some research to see how cohabitation impacts marriage and they find that:
   a. Divorce rates are higher for people that cohabit than those who do not
   b. Divorce rates are lower for people who cohabit than those who do not
   c. There is no difference in the divorce rates of cohabitors and non-cohabit

5. Ted and Mike are a gay couple. They live together and have a sexual relationship. This exemplifies:
   a. Cohabitation
   b. POSSLQs
   c. Both a & b

6. Tim has to do a paper on widowhood and ethnicity. Tim found that _____ women are more likely to be widowed.
   a. African American
   b. White American
   c. American Indian

7. Tracy and Darryl are having a disagreement. Tracy believes that there are more unmarried men than women in America. Darryl believes that there are more unmarried women than men in America. Who is right?
    a. Tracy, there are more unmarried men
    b. Darryl, there are more unmarried women
    c. Neither, there are an equal number of unmarried men & women

8. Thomas is unemployed. Mark works full time. Who is most likely to cohabit?
    a. Thomas
    b. Mark
    c. Employment does not make a difference

9. Cathy is a drug addict. She spends all of her money on drugs so she does not have a place of her own. Over the past year, she has lived with seven different men. She lives with one partner at a time and then moves in with another. This illustrates:
    a. Serial cohabitation
    b. Premarital cohabitation
    c. Trial marriage

10. The sex ratio in China is 118. This means that there are:
    a. Equal numbers of men and women
    b. 118 women for every 100 men
    c. 118 men for every 100 women

11. Harold is a self-sufficient, 28 year old man. He is comfortable washing his own clothes, cooking his own meals, and cleaning his own house. Harold will be single longer than men in previous generations because of changes in:
    a. Gender roles
    b. Demographic
    c. The marriage squeeze

12. Theresa and Winston are dating and they spend all of their free time together. They decide to move in together to maximize how much time they can spend together and minimize rent payments. This illustrates:
    a. Trial marriage
    b. Dating cohabitation
    c. Premarital cohabitation

13. Pauline and Paul are single siblings in their late 50's. Their aging parents need to be cared for, and Pauline cares for them in her home while Paul lives alone. This tendency for older women instead of older men to serve as caretakers reflects the:
    a. Double standard
    b. Sexual standard
    c. Single woman's standard

14. After killing her parents, grandparents, and siblings, Loretta received a prison sentence of 138 years. She will spend the rest of her life behind bars. Although Loretta wanted to remarry, she realizes that she never will. Loretta is which type of single?
    a. Voluntary temporary
    b. Involuntary stable
    c. Involuntary permanent

15. In some parts of Alaska, there are more unmarried men than women. This reflects the:
    a. Sex ratio
    b. Age standard
    c. Marriage squeeze

16. Valentine's Day is approaching and Nicole hopes that her boyfriend proposes to her so that they can get married. She has wanted to get married for the past 3 years and is waiting for him to commit. Nicole is which type of single?
    a. Involuntary stable
    b. Voluntary temporary
    c. Involuntary temporary

17. Twenty years ago, Homer told Marge that he did not need a piece of paper (a marriage license) to prove his commitment to her. They never had a legal marriage, but they have been living together ever since. This illustrates:
    a. Premarital cohabitation
    b. Trial marriage
    c. Substitute marriage

18. Mel and Phil are a gay couple. Alice and Vera are a lesbian couple. Which couple is most likely to be rejected by friends and family?
    a. Mel and Phil
    b. Alice and Vera
    c. They are equally likely

19. Sister Cynthia is a nun, and she will never marry. She is which type of single?
   a. Voluntary stable
   b. Temporary stable
   c. Involuntary stable

20. Phillip is a widowed man, and Lisa is a widowed woman. Which one is more likely to live alone?
   a. Phillip
   b. Lisa
   c. They are equally likely

21. Katrina is a single parent of 8 year old twins. Katrina hopes to marry one day, but only after her children have finished high school and moved out of her house. Katrina is which type of single?
   a. Voluntary stable
   b. Voluntary temporary
   c. Involuntary temporary

22. The year is 1999 and Eileen and Debbie are a lesbian couple. They have decided to move to the state in which the Supreme Court ruled that same sex partners can enter into civil unions. The couple is moving to:
   a. Massachusetts
   b. California
   c. Vermont

23. Rose, Dorothy, and Blanche are three retired elderly women who live together as roommates in a house. This is an example of which form of communal living?
   a. Board and care home
   b. Homesharing
   c. Elderly cottage housing opportunity

24. Tyrone has a drug problem and is irresponsible with money. After living with Renee for 5 months, they get married. Their marriage ends after 2 years. Their break-up is best explained by the:
   a. Cohabitation experience effect
   b. Inertia effect
   c. Selection effect

25. The year is 2003. Lydia is a 24 year old single woman. Lydia wonders if she has passed the median age of marriage for women. Lydia should know that:
   a. Half of all women are younger than she when they marry for the first time
   b. Half of all women are older than she when they marry for the first time
   c. Half of all women are Lydia's age when they marry for the first time.

SELF-ASSESSMENT:
DO YOU SUPPORT SAME-SEX MARRIAGES?

Directions: Read each statement. Put a check in the box to reflect whether or not you agree.

	Agree	Disagree
The military should be able to require military priests and chaplains to perform same-sex marriage ceremonies.		
The commitment experienced by gays and lesbians is just as real as the commitment experienced by heterosexuals.		
Allowing same-sex marriages will reduce the rate of sexually transmitted infections among gays and lesbians.		
Prohibiting same-sex marriages is a form of discrimination.		
Homosexual couples should be allowed the same rights and benefits as heterosexual couples.		
Homosexual couples should be supported in their decision to raise children.		
God approves of same sex marriages.		
The love experienced by gays and lesbians is just as real as the love experienced by heterosexuals.		
Marriage stabilizes homosexual relationships.		
Couples of the same sex deserve society's support for their marriage.		

Key: Give yourself 1 point for every statement that you checked as 'Agree.' A score of 10 represents the most supportive view of same-sex marriage. A score of 0 represents the least supportive view of same sex marriage. A score of 5 represents ambivalence.

ANSWERS

POST-TEST

Answers		Page Numbers
1.	B	276
2.	B	273
3.	C	273
4.	A	276
5.	A	271
6.	C	270
7.	A	264
8.	A	274
9.	A	272
10.	C	264
11.	A	263
12.	B	272
13.	A	260
14.	B	260
15.	C	264
16.	C	260
17.	C	273
18.	A	281
19.	A	259
20.	B	261
21.	B	259
22.	C	282
23.	B	283
24.	C	276
25.	B	258

10

MARRIAGE AND COMMUNICATION IN COMMITTED RELATIONSHIPS

CHAPTER OBJECTIVES

Upon reading Chapter Ten, students should be able to:

1. Explain the reasons why people marry.

2. Describe marriage rituals in the U.S.

3. Compare and contrast the various types of marriage.

4. Discuss the prevalence & characteristics of successful marriages.

5. Explain the relationships between marriage and health.

6. Discuss marital roles in the U.S.

7. Explain how marriages change throughout the life course.

8. Describe the characteristics of effective communication.

9. Compare and contrast sex differences in communication.

10. Discuss common communication problems in relationships.

11. Explain the impact of power and conflict on relationships.

12. Describe how couples use productive communication patterns.

CHAPTER OVERVIEW

Positive motives for marrying increase the likelihood of staying together, while negative reasons derail marriage. Positive motives include: love and companionship, a desire for children, adult identity, commitment, and continuity. Negative reasons include social legitimacy, social pressure, economic security, rebellion, and solution to problems.

Marriage is a rite of passage which involves several major events. An **engagement** formalizes a couple's decision to marry. At a *bridal shower*, female friends and relatives shower a bride with both personal and household gifts and commemorate the beginning of a new partnership. At a *bachelor party*, the groom's friends typically lament their friend's impending loss of freedom and celebrate one last fling. Some women also have *bachelorette parties*. The wedding ceremony typically reinforces the marriage commitment as a sacred, permanent bond. The presence of others affirms the acceptance and legitimacy of the union. About 20% of couples sign prenuptial agreements. There are five different types of marriages: **conflict-habituated marriage** (partners fight but do not believe that this is a reason for divorce), **devitalized marriage** (partners were deeply in love when they married but now spend time together only out of obligation), **passive-congenial marriage** (partners have a low emotional investment and minimal expectations), **vital marriage** (partners' lives are closely intertwined), and **total marriage**, (partners participate in each others lives at all levels and have few areas of tension). The first three types are called *utilitarian marriages* because they are based on convenience; the last two types are called *intrinsic marriages* because the relationships are inherently rewarding. Outside of the U.S., many couples live in LAT (living apart together) relationships.

Researchers usually measure marital success according to marital stability and marital satisfaction. *Marital stability* refers to whether a marriage is intact and whether the spouses have ever suggested divorce to each other. *Marital satisfaction* refers to whether a husband or wife sees their marriage as good. Five aspects of satisfying and stable marriages include compatibility, flexibility, positive attitudes, conflict resolution, and emotional support. Married people are generally healthier and happier than those who are single, divorced, or widowed. The *selection effect* explains that healthy people are attracted to other healthy people and are more desirable marriage partners. The '*protection effect*' suggests that enjoying emotional, social, and physical support from a spouse improves one's general health by reducing anxiety, depression, and risky behaviors. Although married men are healthier than their wives, women live longer than men. The quality of a marriage is much more important to health than simply being married. People who are unhappy in their marriage may experience **marital burnout**, the gradual deterioration of love and ultimate loss of an emotional attachment between marital partners.

When people marry they have certain expectations about their **marital roles,** specific ways that married couples define their behavior and structure their time. Men make fewer adjustments to marriage than women. In the process of **identity bargaining**, newly married partners adjust their idealized expectations to the realities of living together. Gender is the best predictor of marital roles. Wives do 'wifework' to maintain the husband's well-being, but there is no reciprocal 'husbandwork.' Domestic work includes housework and child rearing. Although men's contributions to domestic work have increased, women still do more domestic work than men. Husbands of employed wives tend to do more domestic work than husbands of unemployed wives, unless their wives earn a higher salary. When couples have children, women take on more of the childrearing tasks. Latino and African American men spend more time than whites doing household tasks. The higher a wife's socioeconomic status, the more likely it is that her husband will help with family tasks. Men are happier in their marriages when there is equality in decision making, but not housework. Women are happier when there is equality in decision making and housework.

Throughout the lifecourse, married couples must adjust. Newly married couples adjust to their new roles as husband and wife, to becoming parents, and to the demands of raising children. Mid-life couples adjust to intergenerational ties, relationships with in-laws, the *empty-nest syndrome* (lessened sense of well-being when children leave home), and the **boomerang generation** (young adults who move back in with parents after living independently). Marital satisfaction manifests in a *U shaped curve* over the life course. Couples begin with high levels of satisfaction which later declines after children and then rises when children leave the home. Later-life couples must adjust to retirement and declines in health.

Effective verbal and nonverbal communication is essential to any committed relationship. Major goals of effective communication include 1) developing ways of interacting that are clear, nonjudgmental, and non-punitive, and 2) resolving conflicts through problem solving. **Self-disclosure** is telling another person about one's thoughts and feelings. Reciprocity is important in effective communication and conflict resolution. Disclosure is beneficial when the listener provides esteem support, information support, instrumental support, and motivational support. There are gender differences in communication. Women foster closeness, establish equality, probe for understanding, do conversational maintenance work, offer a personal, concrete style, make references to emotions, and use verbal hedges, disclaimers, fillers and fluences. Men are more likely to show instrumentality, exert control, and demonstrate conversational dominance. Gender roles shape communication. Some men are non-communicative because they believe that they should protect their family. Others feminize their conversations when speaking with their wives. Some of the most common communication problems include: not listening, not responding to the issue at hand, blaming, criticizing and nagging, scapegoating, coercion, and the silent treatment. When partners are not listening, three common miscommunication patterns occur: *cross-complaining*, (spouse presents a complaint without addressing the partner's complaint), *couterproposals* (spouse ignores a partner's suggestion and presents a new one), and *stonewalling* (spouse does not hear or respond to partner).

Power is the ability to impose one's will on others. *Resource theories* suggest that the spouse with more resources has more power in decision making. The *principle of least interest* suggests that the person that is more committed to the marriage has the least power. All partners and families experience conflict, discrete isolated disagreements, or chronic relational problems. The most common disagreements are over money, housework, fidelity, children and privacy. Families tend to use four ways to end conflict: *submission* (one person agrees with or goes along with the other), *compromise* (the partners find a middle ground), *standoff* (partners agree to disagree and move on), and *withdrawal* (one partner refuses to continue the argument). Couples can increase positive communication and decrease negative interaction patterns by asking for information, avoiding generalizations, staying focused, being specific, keeping honesty, being kind, expressing appreciation, and listening. Research on marriage education programs is inconclusive.

PRE-TEST

1. Karen wants a relationship that offers continuity and permanence, so she gets married. Lisa is pregnant and does not want to have a baby outside of wedlock, so she gets married. Which woman is most likely to divorce?
   a. Karen
   b. Lisa
   c. They are equally likely

2. Loretta does a research paper on the marriages depicted on prime time television sitcoms. She finds that most are either vital or total. As such, the shows mostly portray _____ marriages.
   a. Utilitarian
   b. Intrinsic
   c. Practical

3. Richie just asked Laurie Beth to marry him. She said yes! This marks which stage of marriage ritual?
   a. Engagement
   b. Bridal shower
   c. Identity bargaining

4. Kevin and Olivia have been married for 17 years. They live under the same roof, are friendly with one another, are not emotionally invested in the marriage, and have low expectations of one another. Kevin and Olivia are in which type of marriage?
   a. Devitalized
   b. Conflict habituated
   c. Passive-congenial

5. Dino is getting married. His friends grieve over the fact that he is going to lose his freedom. They provide him with one last fling. This marriage ritual is called a:
   a. Bridal party
   b. Groom party
   c. Bachelor party

6. Dhavi and Abdul are a married couple who have been married for 23 years. They fight often but do not believe that fighting is a reason for divorce. Dhavi and Abdul are in which type of marriage?
   a. Conflict-habituated
   b. Devitalized
   c. Passive congenial

7. Joanie and Ralph are getting married. Before the wedding, they sign a contract stating how premarital property should be divided in the event of a divorce. This is called a:
   a. Marriage license
   b. Marriage insurance policy
   c. Prenuptial agreement

8. Jason and Mary were deeply in love when they married 23 years ago. They loved to spend lots of time together back then. Now, the two only spend time together when they absolutely have to. Their marriage is:
   a. Conflict-habituated
   b. Devitalized
   c. Conflict-habituated

9. Okim and Dong have a long distance marriage. She lives on their land in the country and he works in the city. Dong brings Okim money twice a month. Their marriage is a/an _____ relationship.
    a. LAT
    b. RMT
    c. LDR

10. Roseanne and Dan are a married couple that has been married for 12 years. Neither has ever suggested divorce to the other. This suggests that they have:
    a. Marital satisfaction
    b. Marital vitality
    c. Marital stability

11. Sergio thinks that his marriage is bad. As such, Sergio lacks:
    a. Marital stability
    b. Marital satisfaction
    c. Marital vitality

12. Mary Kay and Ashley are 37 year old white, female twins. Mary Kay is married and Ashley is divorced. Who is more likely to be healthy?
    a. Mary Kay
    b. Ashley
    c. They are equally likely

13. Professor Price surveyed his marriage and family class and found that most students want a mate that is healthy. Professor Price informs the class that this prevalent desire for healthy spouses explains health differences by marital status. This illustrates the _____ effect of marriage:
    a. Selection
    b. Protection
    c. Medical power

14. Tammy's love for her husband Leroy has declined over time, and she no longer feels an emotional attachment to him. Tammy is experiencing:
    a. Marital instability
    b. Marital dissatisfaction
    c. Marital burnout

15. In their marriage, Alto pays the bills and Lilly does the housework. This illustrates the couple's:
    a. Gender roles
    b. Sex roles
    c. Marital roles

16. Phillip thought that when he married Vivian, she would come to bed in sexy lingerie every night and that they would have sex at least once every night. Vivian rarely comes to bed in sexy lingerie and they have sex about 3 times a week. The process of Phillip adjusting his ideal expectations to reality is called:
    a. Identity bargaining
    b. Marital negotiation
    c. Role adjustment

17. Mork and Mindy are a married couple. Mindy nurtures her husband Mork by completing physical and emotional tasks to maintain his well-being. This includes cooking his favorite dishes, organizing his social life, and cleaning up after him. This work is also called:
    a. Husbandwork
    b. Wifework
    c. Spousalwork

18. Harry and Carry Fisher are a working married couple. Carry earns $25,000 more per year than Harry. Who is more likely to do the housework in the Fisher household?
    a. Harry
    b. Carry
    c. They are equally likely

19. In the Kowalski marriage, the couple shares equally in decision making, but Mrs. Kowalski does most of the housework. Is Mr. Kowalski or Mrs. Kowalski more likely to be happy with this set-up?
    a. Mr. Kowalski
    b. Mrs. Kowalski
    c. They are equally likely

20. Mercedes and Bentley just had a baby. Which of the following is true?
    a. Their marital satisfaction just increased
    b. Their marital satisfaction just decreased
    c. Their marital satisfaction has not changed

21. Since Pasha and Patina left home after joining the military, their mother Patricia has been depressed. She feels that she no longer has a purpose in life. Patricia is experiencing:
    a. Love nest syndrome
    b. Empty nest syndrome
    c. Boomerang generation syndrome

22. After living with her husband for 6 years, Becky divorced Manny. Becky moved back in with her parents so that she could save some money. Becky is a part of the:
   a. Boomerang generation
   b. Empty nest syndrome
   c. U shaped curve

23. Willis tells his girlfriend about his phobia, or fear of spiders. This revelation of his thoughts and feelings is an example of:
   a. Marital satisfaction
   b. Self-disclosure
   c. Power

24. In their relationship, Harry typically gets his way. He imposes his will on his wife Pauline. This illustrates:
   a. Conflict
   b. Power
   c. Complaining

25. When listening to others, Esther often says "mmh", "ahh" or "unhuh." These words, which cover the conversational gaps of silence, are called:
   a. Verbal fillers
   b. Verbal hedges
   c. References to emotions

EXERCISES/ APPLICATIONS

1.   Imagine that you have inherited your family's wealth and you are about to get married. Develop a mock prenuptial agreement. What areas of marriage would you include and why. How would you feel if your prospective mate asked you sign a premarital contract?

2.   Think of the couples depicted on your favorite television shows. According to the typology presented in the text, which types of marriages are shown? What makes you say so?

CHAPTER 10 KEY TERMS CROSSWORD PUZZLE

Across

7. Generation that returns home
10. Pre-wedding agreement about assets
11. Marital permanence
12. Long distance marriage relationship

Down

1. Revealing personal thoughts
2. The love has declined
3. Identity adjustments
4. Having things your way
5. Formal decision to marry
6. Marital perception is good
8. What each spouse is supposed to do
9. Marriage with obligation
13. Marriage where everything is shared

POST-TEST

1. Jill is on the Board of Directors at the college. Whenever Jill is asked to share her viewpoints, she softens or weakens her statements. She often uses phrases like "I'm not sure, but" or "I may be wrong, but" instead of being more direct. This illustrates the use of:
   a. Verbal hedges
   b. References to emotions
   c. Verbal fillers

2. Mallory tells Jeff that it really bothers her when he makes fun of her cooking in front of the children. By revealing her honest thoughts and feelings, Mallory is engaging in:
   a. Power
   b. Marital satisfaction
   c. Self-disclosure

3. After returning home from the military, Barry moved back in with his parents. This is an example of the:
   a. U shaped curve
   b. Empty nest syndrome
   c. Boomerang generation

4. Jerome and Diara just had a baby. Michelle and James do not have any children. Which couple is likely to have the higher level of marital satisfaction?
   a. Jerome and Diara
   b. Michelle and James
   c. They are equally likely

5. In the Kelsey household, the couple shares equally in the decision making and housework responsibilities. Is Mr. Kelsey or Mrs. Kelsey more likely to be happy with this arrangement?
   a. Mr. Kelsey
   b. Mrs. Kelsey
   c. They are equally likely

6. Sharonda and Kelly are both married women. Sharonda makes $17,000 per year and Kelly makes $87,000 per year. Which of these women is more likely to get help with the housework from her husband?
   a. Sharonda
   b. Kelly
   c. They are equally likely

7. Levi's wife constantly does physical and emotional work to ensure that he is well. This includes ironing his clothes, cooking his food, and massaging his body. This work is called:
   a. Wifework
   b. Husbandwork
   c. Spousalwork

8. Susan thought that once she married Jack that they would have romantic dinners with candlelight and music every night of the week. Yet, Jack rarely comes home for dinner, and when they do have dinner together, it is while watching television. The process of Susan adjusting her ideal expectation to the reality of living with Jack is called:
   a. Marital negotiation
   b. Identity bargaining
   c. Role adjustment

9. In their marriage, Elroy takes care of the yard work and Julie takes care of the children. This explains the couple's:
   a. Sex roles
   b. Marital roles
   c. Gender roles

10. Geraldine no longer feels close to her husband Joe. In fact, her love for him has diminished over the 23 years that they have been together. Geraldine is experiencing:
    a. Marital burnout
    b. Marital dissatisfaction
    c. Marital instability

11. Since he has been married, Paul receives emotional, social, and physical support from his wife. Paul's general health has improved. This is called the _____ effect of marriage:
    a. Medical power
    b. Selection
    c. Protection

12. Brad and Chad are 26 year old white male twins. Brad is married and Chad is a never married single. Who is more likely to healthy?
    a. Chad
    b. Brad
    c. They are equally likely

13. When asked if she thinks that her marriage is good, Margaret said yes. This suggests that Margaret has:
    a. Marital satisfaction
    b. Marital stability
    c. Marital vitality

14. Clair and Cliff raised 5 children. After their youngest daughter Rudy left the house, there was just Clair and Cliff in the home. The couple experienced a period of depression and loneliness. This illustrates the:
    a. Empty nest syndrome
    b. Love nest syndrome
    c. Boomerang generation syndrome

15. Richard and Nicole have been married for 7 years. Last night Richard asked Nicole is she wanted a divorce. This suggests that this couple does not have:
    a. Marital satisfaction
    b. Marital happiness
    c. Marital stability

16. Olga and John are a married couple. They do no get along and argue every single day. In order to save the marriage, John moves out. The two remain married in their separate apartments. This is a/an _____ relationship.
    a. LAT
    b. RMT
    c. LDR

17. Eddie and Sheila have been married for 12 years. They resolve their conflicts through compromise, spend a lot of time together, and make sacrifices for one another. Their marriage is:
    a. Vital
    b. Total
    c. Passive congenial

18. Alfred and Luella are both successful business executives. They decide to marry each other. Before they marry, they sign a contract stating how their savings and checking accounts will be combined. The contract is called a:
    a. Prenuptial agreement
    b. Marriage insurance policy
    c. Marriage license

19. Tiffany is getting married. Her friends had a gathering to celebrate her new partnership. They are providing her with lots of gifts. This marriage ritual is a:
    a. Bridal shower
    b. Bachelorette party
    c. Bridal party

20. Willie and Dorothy have been married for 15 years. They are involved in each other's lives at all levels. They work together, have the same friends, and share in the same hobbies. Their marriage is:
    a. Vital
    b. Passive-congenial
    c. Total

21. Lucuios and Almira are in the stage of marriage ritual that sends a 'hand-off' message to others. Which stage are they in?
    a. Bridal shower
    b. Engagement
    c. Identity bargaining

22. Danita is the single mother of three children, and she wants a husband to help her raise her children. Thomasina wants a husband for intimate companionship. Which woman is most likely to have a stable marriage?
    a. Thomasina
    b. Stephanie
    c. They are equally likely

23. For a class assignment, Wesley examined the types of marriages that are present in his family. He found that the most prevalent types in his family were devitalized, passive-congenial, and conflict habituated. The marriages in Wesley's family are:
    a. Vital
    b. Intrinsic
    c. Utilitarian

24. When Jenny tells her husband Lionel that she likes him to hold her hand when they go for walks, Lionel says that he does not hold her hand because he grew up in a cool family that did not express affection. Which communication problem is illustrated here?
    a. Scapegoating
    b. Blaming
    c. Contempt

25. Samuel and Carla are having an argument over who initiated sex for the first time in their relationship. She says that it was him. He says that it was her. They agree to disagree and move on to other activities. This illustrates
   a. Compromise
   b. Standoff
   c. Withdrawal

SELF-ASSESSMENT:
HOW DOMESTIC ARE YOU?

Directions: Put a circle around four household tasks in each column that you would perform (or are currently performing) in your marriage.

	Column 1	Column 2	Column 3	Column 4
Row 1	Washing Dishes	Laundry	Cooking Indoors	Dusting
Row 2	Taking Out Trash	Mowing the Lawn	Raking the Leaves	Shoveling the Snow
Row 3	Watering Plants	Childcare	Setting Appointments	Organizing Parties
Row 4	Balancing the Checkbook	Paying the Bills	Pruning the Trees	Automobile Maintenance
Row 5	Grocery Shopping	Making Beds	Ironing	Sweeping
Row 6	Making Repairs	Changing Light bulbs	Animal care	Moving Furniture
Row 7	Vacuuming	Setting the Table	Decorating	Mopping
Row 8	Painting	Grilling Outdoors	Lifting/Carrying Heavy Objects	Disciplining children

KEY:

Women	Men
Give yourself 1 point for every chore that you circled in rows 1, 3, 5, and 7. A score of 16 suggests that you are only willing to offer traditionally feminine domestic work to the household. A score of 8 suggests that you are willing to divide the tasks equally with your mate. A score below eight shows a preference for domestic work traditionally done by men.	Give yourself 1 point for every chore that you circled in rows 2, 4, 6, and 8. A score of 16 suggests that you are only willing to offer traditionally masculine domestic work to the household. A score of 8 suggests that you are willing to divide the tasks equally with your mate. A score below eight shows a preference for domestic work traditionally done by women.

ANSWERS

PRE-TEST

Answers	Page Numbers
1. B	289
2. B	294
3. A	291
4. C	294
5. C	291
6. A	294
7. C	193
8. B	294
9. A	195
10. C	295
11. B	293
12. A	298
13. A	299
14. C	300
15. C	300
16. A	301
17. B	301
18. B	302
19. A	302
20. B	305
21. B	306
22. A	306
23. B	308
24. B	311
25. A	309

KEY TERMS CROSSWORD PUZZLE

Across	Page Numbers
7. Boomerang	306
10. Prenuptial	293
11. Stability	295
12. LAT	295

Down	
1. Self-Disclosure	308
2. Marital Burnout	300
3. Bargaining	301
4. Power	311
5. Engagement	291
6. Satisfaction	295
8. Marital role	300
9. Devitalized	294
13. Total	294

POST-TEST

Answers	Page Numbers
1. A	309
2. C	308
3. C	306
4. B	305
5. B	302
6. B	302
7. A	301
8. B	301
9. B	300
10. A	300
11. C	299
12. B	298
13. A	295
14. A	306
15. C	295
16. A	295
17. A	294
18. A	293
19. A	291
20. C	294
21. B	291
22. A	289
23. C	294
24. A	311
25. B	313

11

TO BE OR NOT TO BE A PARENT: MORE CHOICES, MORE CONSTRAINTS

CHAPTER OBJECTIVES

Upon reading Chapter Eleven, students should be able to:

1. Compare and contrast the common reactions to pregnancy.

2. Compare and contrast the benefits and costs of having children

3. Describe how parental lifestyle impacts the health of babies.

4. Explain the effects of parenthood on the mothers and fathers.

5. Discuss fertility patterns in the U.S. and around the world.

6. Explain why people postpone parenthood.

7. Discuss infertility among men and women.

8. Describe patterns of adoption.

9. Compare and contrast medical and high-tech solutions to infertility.

10. Discuss variations in non-marital childbearing.

11. Discuss the prevalence of abortion and abortion laws.

12. Explain why couples choose to be child-free.

CHAPTER OVERVIEW

Couples can be categorized by their reaction to pregnancy: *planners* (jointly decided to conceive and are happy), *acceptance of fate couples* (did not plan it, but are pleasantly surprised), *ambivalent couples* (have mixed feelings), and *yes-no couples* (one partner does not want children).

In the first *trimester* (three month period), the expectant mother may experience frequent nausea, heartburn, insomnia, shortness of breath, painful swelling of the breasts, and fatigue. She may also be concerned about the health of her *fetus* (unborn child from eight weeks until birth). In the second trimester, the mother begins to feel *quickenings (daily movements of the fetus). Sonograms*, diagnostic imaging, can reveal an image of the baby and its sex. Backaches and fatigue are problems at this stage. In the third trimester, a woman may lose interest in sex, retain water, and feel unattractive and clumsy. When vaginal births are not possible, physicians perform a *cesarean section*, (surgical removal of the baby from the womb through the abdominal wall). When parents engage in high-risk behaviors, babies may be born with health problems. Some risks include smoking, alcohol intake, drug use, obesity, and infectious diseases. Chronic drinking leads to **fetal alcohol syndrome** (FAS), a condition characterized by physical abnormalities and mental retardation. Many women experience **postpartum depression**, or 'the blues' after the birth of a baby. This may result from a sudden drop in estrogen and progesterone levels after delivery. Also, high levels of *beta-endorphins*, the body's natural painkillers, drop after birth, and newborn infants need constant care.

Fertility refers to the number of live births in a population. The **total fertility rate (TFR)** measures the average number of children to a woman in a given population. Macro-level changes that explain the decline of the TFR include: improvements in contraceptive methods, more opportunities for women in higher education, advances in medicine and hygiene, and more women in the work force. Micro-level factors include decisions about sex, contraception, and abortion. **Relative income**, a person's earning potential compared with the desired standard of living, also explains declines in fertility rates. Fertility rates are higher among Latinas than other women. Women with more education have fewer children, while women with lower levels space their children closer together. Family size varies around the world because of birth rates. A country needs a 2.1 TFR to replace those who die. **Infant mortality rate** (the number of babies under 1 year of age who die per 1,000 live births in a given year) also impacts family size. Many women are postponing parenthood. Micro-level reasons include not having a mate, economic shortfalls, and the reluctance to give up one's career. Macro level factors include economic recessions and reproductive factors.

Infertility is the inability to conceive a baby after 12 months of unprotected sex. *Idiopathic* infertility is unexplained. Women may be infertile because of a failure to *ovulate* (produce a viable egg each month) or because the *fallopian tubes* (carries the egg from the ovaries to the uterus) are blocked. The fallopian tubes may be blocked by scarring caused by **pelvic inflammatory disease** or PID (an infection of the uterus that spreads to the tubes, ovaries, and surrounding tissue). **Chlamydia** is a sexually transmitted disease that exhibits no symptoms and leads to PID. **Endometriosis**, (the tissue in the lining of the uterus spreads outside the womb) also leads to infertility. Male infertility often results from sluggish sperm or a low sperm count. There are several types of adoption: *public* (child welfare system places child in permanent homes), *private* (private agencies place child in nonrelatives' homes), *kinship* (child placed in relative's home), *stepparent* (child adopted by a birth parent's spouse), *transracial* or *transcultural* (child of one racial or ethnic group is placed with parents of another group), and *international* (citizens of another nation are adopted by U.S. parents). The Multiethnic Placement Act of 1994 makes it illegal to deny transracial adoption. In **open adoption**, information is shared and contact is maintained between biological and adoptive parents. In **closed adoption**, information is confidential and there is no contact. In the **semi-open adoption**, there is communication between the involved parties, but it takes place through a third party. Florida, Mississippi, and Utah banned adoptions by gays and lesbians. The common medical treatments for infertility include **artificial insemination** (semen is artificially introduced into the vagina or uterus near ovulation) and **fertility drugs** (medications that stimulate ovaries to produce eggs). Infertile couples may choose from a variety of **assisted reproductive technology** (any treatment or procedure involving the handling of human eggs and sperm to establish a pregnancy). Some methods are: **in vitro fertilization** or IVF (a woman's eggs are surgically removed, fertilized in a Petri dish and then transferred into her uterus) and **surrogacy** (a woman able to carry a pregnancy to term serves as a substitute for a woman who cannot). **Preimplantation genetic diagnosis** enables physicians to identify genetic diseases in the embryo before implantation so that couples can choose only healthy embryos. Two common prenatal diagnostic procedures are **amniocentesis** (fluid from the amniotic sac is withdrawn and analyzed for abnormalities) and **chorionic villus sampling** (villi are removed from the outer membrane that surrounds the amniotic sac to diagnose abnormalities).

Abortion is the expulsion of the embryo or fetus from the uterus. The *abortion rate*, the number of abortions per 1000 women aged 15 to 44, has declined. The major reason for abortion is financial inability to support a baby. Abortion rates are decreasing because of changing attitudes, contraceptive usage, fewer abortion providers, and policies that cut or limit funds for clinics. Opponents of the morning after pill claim that it is an *abortifacient*, a substance that causes the termination of pregnancy, while proponents claim that they are a form of **contraception**, a method of preventing pregnancy. Abortion has been legal in the U.S. since the Supreme Court's 1973 Roe v. Wade ruling. In 2006, South Dakota passed a law that makes it a felony for a doctor to perform any abortion. In 1979, China instituted a policy allowing every family to have one child. Some women are forced to get abortions and/or undergo sterilization. About 4% of American couples choose not to have children. They prefer to be called "child free" instead of "childless."

PRE-TEST

1. Patricia and Kenny are newlyweds. They decided to conceive a baby and are overjoyed when their son is born. They are:
   . Planners
   . An acceptance of fate couple
   . An ambivalent couple

2. Ray is being raised in foster care. Sol is being raised by adoptive parents. Which child is more likely to complete high school?
   . Ray
   . Sol
   . They are equally likely

3. Doctors inform Sherry that she is infertile. Her body fails to produce a viable egg every month. Sherry fails to:
   . Ovulate
   . Menstruate
   . Fallopiate

4. Ruth is pregnant. Warren, Ruth's husband noticed that his wife has lost interest in sex. Ruth is in which trimester?
   . 1st
   . 2nd
   . 3rd

5. The year is 2006. Dr. Wong lives in the state that passed a law making it a felony for doctors to perform abortions. Dr. Wong lives in:
   . South Dakota
   . Florida
   . Mississippi

6. The doctors do not know why Muhammad and Amina are infertile. This type of infertility is:
   . Undiagnosed
   . Idiopathic
   . Pathological

7. Valerie and Ernest are a married couple. When Valerie finds out that she is pregnant, the couple is pleasantly surprised. They are:
   . Planners
   . An acceptance of fate couple
   . An ambivalent couple

8. Zipporah is a pregnant woman who drinks vodka every day. Chances are great that Zipporah's baby will be born with:
   . Fetal alcohol syndrome
   . Down's syndrome
   . Blindness

9. Stephanie and Neal put their child Ormond up for adoption 7 years ago. A social worker mediates communication between these biological parents and their child. This illustrates which type of adoption?
   . Semi-open
   . Open
   . Closed

10. Iola is pregnant. Today, she is going to have a sonogram to learn the sex of her baby. Which trimester is Iola in?
    . 1st
    . 2nd
    . 3rd

11. Marquita is ready to deliver her baby. Because of complications, the doctors must surgically remove the baby though the abdominal wall. Marquita is having a/an:
    . Vaginal birth
    . Cesarean section
    . Abortion

12. Edna is unable to carry a baby to full term, so her sister Nina serves as a substitute. Nina is artificially inseminated with sperm from Edna's husband. Nina is:
    . A surrogate
    . An Assisted Reproductive Unit (ARU)
    . In vitro

1. When Kimberly found out that she was pregnant, she was sad because she did not want a baby. Her husband Todd was overjoyed because he wanted a baby. The couple had the baby because Todd felt so strongly. They are:
   . An acceptance of fate couple
   . An ambivalent couple

. A yes-no couple

14. The year is 2006. Ben and Jerry are a gay couple. They would like to adopt a baby but the law in their state bans gays and lesbians from adopting babies. Ben & Jerry live in:
   . Florida
   . Alabama
   . Georgia

15. Beatriz experienced the blues after having her baby. She was very sad and did not even want to hold the baby. Beatriz had:
   . Maternal deficiency
   . Maternal schizophrenia
   . Post-partum depression

16. China has a TFR of 1.2. Which of the following is true?
   a. The country is replacing its dying members
   b. The country is not replacing its dying members
   . None of the above

17. Seven out of every 1,000 babies born in America die. This tells us the _____ rate.
   . Fertility
   . Infant mortality
   . Total fertility

18. George and Jane Jetson do not make enough money to buy the house or car that they desire. This reflects their:
   . Financial ability
   . Relative income
   . Economic status

2. Tabitha has been diagnosed with the sexually transmitted disease that exhibits no symptoms but often results in infertility. Tabitha has:
   . Syphilis
   . Herpes
   . Chlamydia

3. George and Nancy Pappadapolous are a white American couple. They adopt Webster, an African-American child. This adoption is:
   . International
   . Transracial
   . Both a & b

21. Ophelia and Sophia are sisters. Ophelia makes $62,000 per year and Sophia makes $26,000 per year. Which woman is likely to have the greatest number of children?
   . Ophelia
   . Sophia
   . They are equally likely

22. Havana is 38 and Lupe is 18. Which woman is more likely to have a baby with a birth defect?
   . Havana
   . Lupe
   . They are equally likely

23. Winnie and Nelson want to know the sex of the baby that Winnie is carrying. They can find out through:
   . A Cesarean section
   . A Sonogram
   . Amniocentesis

24. Keisha was adopted by the Browns, but she maintains contact with her birth parents. This reflects which type of adoption?
   . Open
   . Closed
   . Semi-open

4. Doctors removed eggs from Dorothy's ovaries, fertilized them in a Petri dish with her husband's sperm, and then put the embryo into her uterus. This procedure is known as:
   . Artificial insemination
   . Amniocentesis
   . In vitro fertilization

EXERCISES/ APPLICATIONS

1. Opponents of morning after pills say they are abortifacients, substances that terminate pregnancy, while proponents claim that they are contraceptives, methods to prevent pregnancy. In your view, are they abortifacients or contraceptives? Why?

2. Engage your family members in a conversation about the pros and cons of having children. Then, deliberately take the point of view that although you plan to marry, you would like to *remain childfree.* Your family's response may prove to be an excellent real-life illustration of the pressure that Americans feel to parent and the stereotypes associated with childfree adults.

CHAPTER 11 KEY TERMS CROSSWORD PUZZLE

Across
4. STI leading to infertility
6. Inability to have a baby
9. Average # of babies per woman
10. Ailment causing infertility
11. Fertilization in a Petri dish

Down
1. Depression following the baby
2. Spreading of uterus lining
3. Medicines aiding conception
4. Way to prevent pregnancy
5. Adoption based on confidentiality
7. Result of drinking while pregnant
8. Substitute baby bearer
12. Adoption with info sharing

POST-TEST

1. Min is infertile. The tissue in the lining of Min's uterus spread outside of her womb. This condition is known as:
   . Pelvic inflammatory disease
   . Chlamydia
   . Endometriosis

2. Luigi does not want children and his wife Angela tells him not to worry because she is taking birth control pills. However, Angela does not take the pills because she wants a baby. The couple conceives a child. They are:
   . An acceptance of fate couple
   . An ambivalent couple
   . A yes-no couple

3. Afghanistan has a TFR of 6.8. Which of the following is true?
   a. The country is replacing its dying members
   b. The country is not replacing its dying members
   . None of the above

4. Taylor was adopted by the Foresters. She has no information about her birth parents and they have no information about her. This reflects a/an _____ adoption.
   . Open
   . Closed
   . Semi-open

5. Both Monica and Chandler have been tested. Yet doctors are unable to find out why the couple is infertile. This type of infertility is:
   . Idiopathic
   . Pathological
   . Undiagnosed

6. Ed and Faith are white Americans who adopted a Chinese baby from Asia. Which type of adoption is this?
   . Transracial
   . International
   . Both a &b

7. After 6 months of having unprotected sex without conception, Brian and Marsha wonder if they are infertile. The doctor tells them:
   . They are
   . They are not
   . It is too soon to tell

8. Enrique is 42 and Ramon is 22. Which man probably is more likely to have the resources needed to raise a child?
   . Enrique
   . Ramon
   . They are equally likely

2. Wendy is a single parent. She would like to send her children to private school, involve them on little league baseball teams, and take annual family vacations. She is not able to do these things on her salary. This inability to achieve the desired standard of living reflects:
   . Economic status
   . Financial inability
   . Relative income

10. Today, physicians will withdraw fluid from Sonia's amniotic sac to determine if her baby has Down's syndrome or spina bifida. This procedure is called:
    . Chorionic villus sampling
    . Cesarean section
    . Amniocenteses

11. On average, there are 1.2 children born per woman in South Korea. This tells us the _____ rate.
    . Fertility
    . Infant mortality
    . Total fertility

12. After having her baby, Polly was depressed. She did not want to get out of bed. Polly was experiencing:
    . Schizophrenia
    . Maternal deficiency
    . Post-partum depression

13. Karen is pregnant. Lately, she has been feeling quickenings, or movements by her fetus. She is in which trimester?
    . 1st
    . 2nd
    . 3rd

14. Doug and Katherine are having a baby. The doctor tells them that through the results of _____, they can find out the sex of the baby.
    . A Sonogram
    . Amniocentesis
    . Cesarean section

15. Rachel is a pregnant woman who has untreated syphilis. Chances are great that Rachel's baby will be born with:
    a. Down's syndrome
    b. Fetal alcohol syndrome
    . Blindness

16. Tara is pregnant. She experiences nausea and heartburn often. Which trimester is Tara in?
    . 1st
    . 2nd
    . 3rd

17. Michelle has an appointment to have her baby on the 17th of March. Her cousin asks how an exact delivery date is possible in advance. Michelle tells her that the physicians are scheduled to remove the baby through the vaginal walls on that date. Michelle is having a/an
    . Vaginal birth
    . Cesarean section
    . Abortion

18. Keinu is infertile. She had a sexually transmitted disease that caused pelvic inflammatory disease and now her fallopian tubes are blocked. Keinu had:
    . Herpes
    . Syphilis
    . Chlamydia

19. Heather is a teenage mother. Heather does not believe that she will be a good mother for her son, so she gives him up for adoption. However, she wants to know how he is doing every so often, so she calls a social worker who provides her with information. This reflects which type of adoption:
    . Open
    . Semi-open
    . Closed

3. Gwen underwent a medical procedure during which semen was placed in her vagina at the time of ovulation. This procedure is called:
    . In vitro fertilization
    . Artificial insemination
    . Amniocentesis

21. Leon and Brenda do not want to conceive a baby. To prevent pregnancy, they use condoms. Condoms are an example of:
    . Contraceptives
    . Abortifacients

. Both a & b

22. Over dinner, 2 couples argue over the Supreme Court's 1973 Roe v. Wade decision. One couple strongly supports it and the other strongly opposes it. The Roe v. Wade decision:
    . Banned abortion in the U.S.
    . Legalized abortion in the U.S
    . Set penalties for doctors performing abortions in the U.S.

23. Demetria and Benson choose not to have children. They prefer to be called:
    . Childless
    . Child free
    . Barren

4. Mandy is ten weeks pregnant and she is worried about whether her baby is healthy. Mandy has decided that she will abort the baby if there are any problems. Which test is available now to determine if Mandy's baby has Down's syndrome?
    . Amniocentesis
    . sonogram
    . chorionic villus sampling

25. Jason and Maggie are newlyweds. They do not use any form of birth control. When the couple learns that Maggie is pregnant, they are pleasantly surprised. They are:
    . Planners
    . An acceptance of fate couple
    . An ambivalent couple

SELF-ASSESSMENT:
DO YOU REALLY WANT CHILDREN?

Directions: Read each statement. Put a check in the box to reflect whether or not you agree.

	Agree	Disagree
It is a joy to watch children grow.		
I have so much love to share with a child.		
I would feel incomplete if I died before having children.		
Children will offer me a chance to leave a legacy.		
It is every person's responsibility to have children.		
Only children are able to turn a couple into a family.		
With children, I would not have to worry about who would care for me in my old age.		
Children are worth every sacrifice that parents make.		
I am to provide economically for a child.		
I am a good caretaker.		
Children are fun!		
Children provide adults with the ability to relive their childhood.		
I have the patience needed to raise children		
I can handle the responsibility of having a child.		
I have the energy needed to raise children.		
Children make life more satisfying.		
I would be shirking my duty if I did not have children.		
Children strengthen the relationship between their parents.		
Having a child would make me happy.		
Being a parent is one of the most fulfilling roles one can have.		

Key: Give yourself one point for each statement that you checked as 'Agree.' A score of 20 represents a person who certainly wants to have children. A score of 0 represents a person who definitely <u>does not</u> want children. A score of 10 represents a person who is ambivalent.

ANSWERS

PRE-TEST

Answers		Page Numbers
1.	A	320
2.	C	334
3.	A	330
4.	C	321
5.	A	346
6.	B	330
7.	B	320
8.	A	322
9.	A	333
10.	B	321
11.	B	322
12.	A	338
13.	B	320
14.	A	333
15.	C	323
16.	B	324
17.	A	324
18.	B	325
19.	C	330
20.	B	332
21.	B	325
22.	A	329
23.	B	321
24.	A	333
25.	C	337

KEY TERMS CROSSWORD PUZZLE

Across	Page Numbers
4. Chlamydia	330
6. Infertility	330
9. TFR	324
10. PID	330
11. In vitro	337

Down	
1. Post-partum	323
2. Endometriosis	331
3. Fertility Drugs	336
4. Contraception	342
5. Closed	333
7. FAS	322
8. Surrogate	338
12. Open	333

POST-TEST

Answers		Page Numbers
1.	C	331
2.	C	320
3.	A	324
4.	B	333
5.	A	330
6.	C	332
7.	C	330
8.	A	329
9.	C	325
10.	C	339
11.	C	324
12.	C	323
13.	B	321
14.	A	321
15.	C	322
16.	A	321
17.	B	322
18.	C	344
19.	B	333
20.	B	336
21.	A	342
22.	B	345
23.	B	347
24.	C	339
25.	B	320

RAISING CHILDREN: PROMISES AND PITFALLS

CHAPTER OBJECTIVES

Upon reading Chapter Twelve, students should be able to:

1.   Explain the role strain experienced by parents.

2.   Compare and contrast ideal and realistic roles for parents.

3.   Compare and contrast theories of child development.

4.   Compare and contrast parenting styles.

5.   Discuss parental discipline.

6.   Discuss variations in parenting across racial-ethnic families.

7.   Discuss variations in parenting across social class.

8.   Discuss parenting over the life course.

9.   Discuss parenting in lesbian and gay families.

10.   Describe how parents impact children's development.

11.   Discuss various child care arrangements and how they impact families.

12.   Explain how electronic media impact children's well-being.

13.   Discuss problems associated with foster homes.

CHAPTER OVERVIEW

Most parents face **role strain**, or conflict felt within a role. Parental role strain is shaped by unrealistic role expectations, decreased authority, increased responsibility, and high parenting standards. Many people believe that mothering comes naturally. This belief is problematic because it creates unrealistic expectations and stereotypes. There are three types of contemporary fathers: *breadwinner* (views fatherhood mainly in economic terms and prefers a wife who takes care of domestic life), *autonomous* (seeks freedom from family commitments) and *involved* (participates extensively in daily tasks of child rearing and nurturing).

Mead's Theory of the social self views the *self* as the basis of humanity and suggests that self develops out of social interactions. The infant is a blank slate (*tabula rasa*) with no behavioral predispositions. By interacting with others, the infant develops attitudes, beliefs, and behaviors. Piaget's cognitive development theory suggests that children play an active role in learning, processing information, and seeking knowledge. All children must pass through four stages, and once children have mastered the tasks of one stage, they move on to the next, more difficult stage. Erikson's psychosocial theory of development suggests that humans develop over the lifespan in eight stages. In each stage, the person faces a specific crisis that presents tasks and risks.

A **parenting style** is a general approach to interacting with and disciplining children. *Support* refers to the amount of affection, acceptance, warmth, and caring that parents provide. *Control* is the degree of flexibility a parent exhibits in guiding a child's behavior. There are four parenting styles: **authoritarian** (demanding, rigid, and punitive), **permissive** (warm, responsive, and undemanding), **authoritative** (demanding, responsive, and supportive), and **uninvolved** (indifferent). Healthy child development is most likely in authoritative family settings. Children must learn discipline because self-control is not innate. Almost all parents use verbal and psychological aggression to control their children's behavior. Even more, 94% of all parents spank their children by the time they are 3 or 4 years old. Research suggests that corporal punishment increases children's aggression and misbehavior.

Latino parents are least likely to read to their children. White children under 12 years of age experience more outings than black and Latino children. Black and Latino fathers tend to supervise their children's activities more than white fathers. **Socioeconomic status** (SES) is an overall rank of one's position based on income, education, and occupation. Low SES parents give infants fewer opportunities for daily stimulation and appropriate play materials. Middle SES mothers talk to infants more and in more sophisticated ways than do low SES mothers. They also seek professional advice about child development. High SES parents read more to their children and provide more outings.

The first year of a child's life can be very demanding as infants need 'continuous coverage.' Infancy is a period of extreme helplessness and enormous physical and cognitive growth. During this period, parents are stressed and fatigued and may face insecurity. Parents can protect themselves by being aware of myths that create unnecessary anxiety. The quality of relationships with adults and caregivers impacts child development. Employed parents often face **role overload**, a feeling of being overwhelmed by multiple commitments. The *empty-nest stage* is the period when parents, typically in their 50s, find themselves alone at home after children have left the home. A growing international phenomenon is the *boomerang generation*, young adults who move back in with their parents after living independently. Most parents provide some form of help to at least one of their adult children. Many grandparents are raising grandchildren.

Gay and lesbian parents are raising children who will often experience discrimination because of their parents' sexual orientation. Children in gay families do not differ much in their peers and other social relationships when compared to those raised in heterosexual families. When children reveal that they are gay or lesbian to their heterosexual parents, the response is typically negative because parents think that their children could be heterosexual if they wanted to.

Parents are responsible for teaching children the difference between right and wrong and establishing routines and rituals. Most parents are responsible and have a positive impact on their children. Parents' negative impact may involve *acts of commission* (irresponsible behavior) and *acts of omission* (the absence of responsible behaviors).

Absentee fathers negatively affect children through economic deprivation and lack of social support. Families in which both parents are employed full time are called **DEWKS**, or dual employed with kids. The number of **latchkey kids**, children who go home after school to unsupervised homes, is growing. Most children under age 5 with employed parents are in some form of nonparental care each week. Most parents are concerned about abuse and neglect in day care centers.

The typical American child is saturated with electronic media. Children who watch a lot of television tend to do poorly in school and begin drinking alcohol at earlier ages. The growth of poverty, child abuse, and parental neglect has increased out-of-home placements for children. The most common placement is in a **foster home**, where parents raise children who are not their own. Many children go through multiple placements and remain in foster care until late adolescence. The typical foster parent is paid very little.

PRE-TEST

1. David faces conflict within his role as a father. He has a lot of responsibility to ensure that his children know right from wrong, but he does not feel that he has the needed authority to enforce his ideas. This conflict represents:
   a. Role strain
   b. Role conflict
   c. Role overload

2. Ricardo is the father of two boys. He believes that being a good father means being involved in the daily tasks of child rearing and nurturing. Which type of father is Ricardo?
   a. Autonomous
   b. Breadwinner
   c. Involved

3. Tonya believes that her daughter is a blank slate. She is very careful about the social interaction that she allows her daughter to partake in because she believes that each interaction will impact her daughter's 'self.' Which theory does Tonya subscribe to?
   a. Mead's theory of social self
   b. Piaget's cognitive development theory
   c. Erikson's psychosocial theory of development

4. Debra is a fifth grade teacher. During parent-teacher meeting day, Debra notices that the parents of her students have various approaches to interacting with and disciplining children. The parents have different:
   a. Parenting styles
   b. Parenting support
   c. Parenting control

5. Meredith keeps her children on a diet of pre-sweetened cereals and Ramen noodles. Because of Meredith's failure to provide proper nutrition, her children are not very healthy. This reflects:
   a. An act of commission
   b. An act of omission
   c. Both a & b

6. While at the barbershop, Eugene overhears a conversation. The men are talking about Eugene's son. It seems that Eugene's son has won a state chess championship. Eugene did not even know that his son knew how to play chess. Which type of parent is Eugene?
   a. Uninvolved
   b. Permissive
   c. Rejecting

7. Irene is an 84 year old social scientist. She has 5 children. According to Irene, she has watched her oldest child pass through the eight stages of human development. Which theory does Irene subscribe to?
   a. Mead's theory of social self
   b. Piaget's cognitive development theory
   c. Erikson's psychosocial theory of development

8. Esther and Bowie are the parents of three children. Their children describe them as affectionate, accepting, warm, and caring. This responsiveness refers to which aspect of parenting style:
   a. Affection
   b. Control
   c. Support

9. Tamika and Wayne are the parents of three. They expect absolute obedience to their commands, with no questions asked. When they say jump, they expect their children to say, "How high?" Tamika and Wayne are:
   a. Authoritarian
   b. Authoritative
   c. Permissive

10. Addie and Regan use corporal punishment to discipline their 3 children. Ty and Lin do not. Which parents are more likely to have aggressive children?
    a. Addie and Regan
    b. Ty and Lin
    c. They are equally likely

11. Clair and Cliff raised 5 children. After their youngest daughter Rudy left the house, there was just Clair and Cliff in the home. The couple experienced a period of depression and loneliness. This illustrates the:
    a. Empty nest syndrome
    b. Love nest syndrome
    c. Boomerang generation

12. After school, Nabeel goes home to an empty house. He lets himself in, fixes a snack, completes his homework, and plays video games until his parents come home. Nabeel is a:
    a. Boomeranger
    b. Latch-key kid
    c. DEWKs

13. Robert realizes that he has a higher income, more education, and a more prestigious occupation than his father. Robert has a higher:
    a. Position
    b. Socioeconomic status
    c. Relative Income

14. Paul is a husband, father, executive, baseball coach, and lodge member. Sometimes, Paul is overwhelmed by these multiple commitments. This is called:
    a. Role conflict
    b. Role strain
    c. Role overload

15. Since divorcing his wife, Willie has not called once to see how his children are doing, and he does not send any money for child support. Willie is which type of father?
    a. Breadwinner
    b. Autonomous
    c. Involved

16. Alonzo and Lisa are the parents of 2 young girls. They believe that their children should be happy at all times. As such, they provide their children with whatever they ask for, and they do not require their children to do chores. Alonzo and Lisa are:
    a. Uninvolved
    b. Permissive
    c. Rejecting

17. After living with her husband for 6 years, Becky divorced Alvin. Becky moved back in with her parents so that she could save some money. This describes the:
    a. Boomerang generation
    b. Empty nest syndrome
    c. U shaped curve

18. Marvin has smoked marijuana in front of his son John since John was an infant. John begins to smoke marijuana when he is 11 years old. Marvin's behavior is:
    a. An act of omission
    b. An act of commission
    c. Both a & b

19. Reggie and Tia are the proud parents of 2 children. Both parents have full time-jobs. As such, they are called:
    a. DEWKS
    b. Latchkey parents
    c. Boomerang parents

20. Joe is a plumber who works about 60 hours per week. He sees his job as a father as an economic one. He believes that he is a 'good dad' because he pays the bills. He leaves the childrearing and homemaking to his wife. Which type of dad is Joe?
    a. Involved
    b. Autonomous
    c. Breadwinner

21. Brooke is a teenager in high school. She bullies the other students and often cuts class to get high. Brooke's parents probably had which parenting style?
    a. Authoritarian
    b. Permissive
    c. Uninvolved

22. Frank and Tina have one child and they are expecting another. Research suggests that raising the 2nd child will be:
    a. Less difficult than the 1st child
    b. More difficult than the 1st child
    c. Equal to the difficulty of the 1st child.

23. Claudette and Gwen are a lesbian couple raising children. Brian and Rochelle are a heterosexual couple raising children. Which couple is more likely to spank their children?
    a. Claudette and Gwen
    b. Brian and Rochelle
    c. They are equally likely

24. Upon entering first grade, Miles is 15 pounds overweight. Which parenting style contributes to obesity in children?
    a. Uninvolved
    b. Authoritarian
    c. Permissive

25. The Kowalsakis are raising children who are not their own. They receive a monthly stipend which covers some costs. The Kowalsakis have a:
   a. Foster home
   b. Child care center
   c. Both a & b

EXERCISES/ APPLICATIONS

1. Which style of parenting did your parents use in their relationship with you? Do you plan to use the same style with your children? Why or why not?

2. Think about your favorite family television shows. Is the myth that mothering comes naturally supported? Are the fathers portrayed as breadwinners, autonomous, or involved?

3. Mothers are more involved in childrearing than fathers. Create a list which shows the childrearing tasks that you think that mothers should handle and the childrearing tasks that fathers should handle. Which personal beliefs shape your list?

CHAPTER 12 KEY TERMS CROSSWORD PUZZLE

Across

3. Conflict within a role
9. Demanding & punitive parent
10. Both parents clock 40 hours per week
11. Parent's approach to children
12. Ranking of societal position

Down

1. They go home to an empty home
2. Blank Slate
4. After children leave the home
5. Where parents raise unrelated kids
6. Indifferent parent
7. Indulgent & undemanding parent
8. Generation that returns home
9. Demanding & supportive parent

POST-TEST

1. Minneola is currently being raised by the Livingstons, although they are not her parents. The Livingstons receive a monthly stipend to take care of Minneola in their:
   a. Child care center
   b. Foster home
   c. Both a & b

2. Roseanne and Dan are a married couple. They have 3 children. Roseanne works 40 hours a week at a factory and Dan works 60 hours a week in construction. This couple represents:
   a. DEWKS
   b. Latchkey parents
   c. Boomerang generation

3. Katrina is thinking about placing her 4 year old son in a child care center. She wonders if her child would have a greater likelihood of being abused. Katrina should know that:
   a. Children are more likely to be abused by day-care workers than relatives
   b. Children are more likely to be abused by relatives than day-care workers
   c. Children are equally likely to be abused by day care workers and relatives.

4. Theodore has never read to his son Richie. Richie is in the 7th grade and hates reading. He is not doing well in school. This illustrates an:
   a. Act of omission
   b. Act of commission
   c. Both a & b

5. Since Pasha and Patina left home after joining the military, their mother Patricia has been depressed. She feels that she no longer has a purpose in life. Patricia is experiencing:
   a. Love nest syndrome
   b. Boomerang generation
   c. Empty nest syndrome

6. Sky is a business owner, a mother, a wife, caretaker for her mother, and a Girl Scout troop leader. Sometimes, she feels overwhelmed by her many commitments. Sky is experiencing:
   a. Role strain
   b. Role conflict
   c. Role overload

7. Maria is Latina. Shequetta is African American. Both girls are 7 years old. Which one is most likely to be read to by her parents?
   a. Maria
   b. Shequetta
   c. They are equally likely

8. Dominique and Nikki are the parents of two teenagers. Although the parents impose rules and standards about homework, chores, and curfew, they are very supportive of their children. This couple's parenting style is:
   a. Authoritarian
   b. Permissive
   c. Authoritative

9. To celebrate his son's 16th birthday, Mr. Montana hired a stripper for the party. Among other things, Mr. Montana sent his child a negative message about women as sex objects. This reflects an act of:
   a. Commission
   b. Omission
   c. Both a & b

10. Nathaniel is an 84 year old social scientist. He visits his deceased wife's gravesite once every 10 years in the old country. During his visits, he 'updates' her on their only child. This year, he tells her that their child has finally passed through the eight stages of human development. Which theory does Nathaniel subscribe to?
    a. Mead's theory of social self
    b. Piaget's cognitive development theory
    c. Erikson's psychosocial theory of development

11. Michelle is a poor single mother. Renee is an upper class single mother. Which one is more likely to want her child to get a college education?
    a. Michelle
    b. Renee
    c. They are equally likely

12. Walter and Lanita are the parents of twin girls. Their daughters would describe them as demanding and inflexible. These characteristics describe which aspect of parenting style?
    a. Affection
    b. Control
    c. Support

13. Floyd is in the 5th grade. After school, Floyd goes home to an empty house. He typically lets himself in and goes on-line to visit pornographic websites. Floyd is a:
    a. Latch-key kid
    b. Boomeranger
    c. DEWKs

14. Manny usually takes the trash out. Today, he tells his son to do it. His son asks why and Manny replies, "Because I said so." Manny expects his son to obey him without question. This reflects which style of parenting?
    a. Authoritative
    b. Authoritarian
    c. Uninvolved

15. Jack has a son and keeps a journal of his child's growth and development. Jack believes that his son's development involves passing through four increasingly difficult stages. Which theory does Jack subscribe to?
    a. Mead's theory of social self
    b. Piaget's cognitive development theory
    c. Erikson's psychosocial theory of development

16. Kevin is a deadbeat dad. He has distanced himself from his wife and his children. In fact, Kevin does not even know where they live, and he does not want to know. Which type of father is Kevin?
    a. Breadwinner
    b. Autonomous
    c. Involved

17. Marina is facing conflict within her role as a mother. While she has had no formal preparation for motherhood, she is expected to be a super mom. This conflict represents:
    a. Role strain
    b. Role conflict
    c. Role overload

18. Al and Peg Bundy are indifferent to their children. They seldom know where they are or who they are with. Frankly, they do not care. These parents are:
    a. Authoritarian
    b. Rejecting
    c. Uninvolved

19. Jaquay and Lamont are the parents of 2 adult women. Marva and Leon are the parents of 2 adult sons. Which parents are more likely to experience the boomerang generation returning to their home?
    a. Jaquay and Lamont
    b. Marva and Leon
    c. They are equally likely

20. Clinton is the father of a 5 year old. Although he home-schools his daughter, he involves her in weekly play groups with other children. Clinton believes that his daughter needs social interactions with others to help her learn necessary behaviors, attitudes, and beliefs. Clinton subscribes to which theory?
    a. Mead's theory of social self
    b. Piaget's cognitive development theory
    c. Erikson's psychosocial theory of development

21. After returning home from the military, Barry moved back in with his parents. This is an example of the:
    a. U shaped curve
    b. Empty nest syndrome
    c. Boomerang generation

22. Macy was very poor growing up. She had a very hard life. Now that she is rich, she wants her children to have the life that she wanted when she was a child. Her children do not have to do any chores and they get whatever gifts they want. Macy's parenting style is:
    a. Authoritarian
    b. Uninvolved
    c. Permissive

23. Phoebe and Rachel are a lesbian couple raising children. Monica and Chandler are a heterosexual couple raising children. Which couple is more likely to spank their children?
    a. Phoebe and Rachel
    b. Monica and Chandler
    c. They are equally likely

24. Dana and Olivia are debating about the benefits and consequences of having children over the age of 50. Which of the following is true?
    a. Older parents are more likely than younger parents to use corporal punishment
    b. Older parents are less likely than younger parents to use corporal punishment
    c. Older parents and younger parents are equally likely to use corporal punishment

25. Edward is a father. He believes that it is his responsibility to provide for the family while his wife tends to the domestic tasks. Which type of father is Edward?
   a. Breadwinner
   b. Autonomous
   c. Involved

SELF-ASSESSMENT: WHAT IS YOUR PARENTING STYLE?

Directions: Put a check in the box to reflect whether or not you agree.

		Agree	Disagree
1	Children need discipline that hurts a little so that they will remember the lesson later.		
2	It is best to give children what they want to protect the peace.		
3	Parents should not use harsh punishment.		
4	If parents provide a good environment, children will pretty much raise themselves		
5	Children must know that the parent is boss.		
6	Children must know that their parents will give them what they want.		
7	Children must know that their parents will hear them out.		
8	Children must know that they are on their own.		
9	Too many children today talk back to their parents when they should just quietly obey them		
10	You can never do too much for your child.		
11	When children present a valid point, parents should consider changing the rules.		
12	Most parents give their children too much attention.		
13	"Spare the rod and spoil the child" is still the best policy.		
14	Children have the last word about what they will do.		
15	Children need to have clear expectations.		
16	Parents do not need to know where their children are.		
17	Children need to have chores in the home.		
18	Parents should do everything to make children happy.		
19	Children should be praised for following the rules.		
20	Children don't need much supervision.		

Key: Circle the numbers that match the statements that you marked as 'agree' in the boxes below. Your parenting style matches the one with the most circled numbers.

Authoritarian	Permissive	Authoritative	Uninvolved
1, 5, 9, 13, 17	2, 6, 10, 14, 18	3, 7, 11, 15, 19	4, 8, 12, 16, 20

ANSWERS

POST-TEST

Answers		Page Numbers
1.	B	380
2.	A	376
3.	B	377
4.	A	374
5.	C	371
6.	C	370
7.	B	361
8.	C	358
9.	A	374
10.	C	357
11.	C	363-364
12.	C	357
13.	A	376
14.	B	357
15.	B	355
16.	B	354
17.	A	352
18.	C	358
19.	B	371
20.	A	355
21.	C	371
22.	C	358
23.	B	373
24.	B	360
25.	A	354

13
BALANCING WORK & FAMILY LIFE

CHAPTER OBJECTIVES

Upon reading Chapter Thirteen, students should be able to:

1.   Explain how economic factors affect family life.

2.   Compare and contrast the different types of poverty and explain why poverty persists.

3.   Discuss the demographic characteristics of and reasons for homelessness.

4.   Describe employment techniques used by the poor.

5.   Compare and contrast the different types of working mothers.

6.   Describe the division of labor in marriages.

7.   Compare and contrast the different types of dual earner families.

8.   Explain how working impacts family life.

9.   Discuss gender inequality in the work place.

10.   Discuss how work-place policies impact families.

CHAPTER OVERVIEW

A *social class* is a category of people who have a similar rank based on wealth, education, power, and prestige. **Wealth** is the money and economic assets that a person owns. **Income** is the amount of money a person receives, usually through wages or salaries. Income inequality in the U.S. is greater than in any other Western industrialized nation. The rich are getting richer, the middle classes are struggling, and the poor have gotten poorer. Macro-level factors that have negatively impacted working-class families include: technological changes that have replaced manual workers with machines, *offshoring* (the relocation of U.S. manufacturers to developing countries), structural changes in the economy which replaced production jobs with low paying service work, and more support for **corporate welfare** (governmental assistance to businesses) instead of assistance to the poor. There are two ways to define poverty: **absolute poverty** (unable to afford the basic necessities of life) and **relative poverty** (inability to maintain an average standard of living). The **poverty line** is the minimal level of income that the federal government considers necessary for individuals' and families' basic subsistence. The poverty line is determined by multiplying 3 times the annual cost of minimum-nutrient level food. Children, the elderly, women, and racial-ethnic minorities are disproportionately poor. The **feminization of poverty** describes the growing proportion of women and their children who are poor. This is explained by unmarried teen mothers having little *human capital* (work-related assets), desertion, and divorce. Almost 40% of all workers are considered **working poor**, people who spend at least 27 weeks a year in the labor force but have incomes below the official poverty level. The functions of poverty and inequality include: the poor ensures that society's dirty work gets done; they subsidize the middle and upper classes by working for low wages; they buy goods and services that would otherwise be rejected; and they absorb the costs of societal change and community growth. Families are the fastest-growing group of homeless people. One of the main reasons for homelessness is the lack of affordable housing. Many families have adopted employment techniques to survive economic changes. These include taking low-paying jobs, moonlighting, working shifts, doing part-time work, and working overtime. Unemployment figures are artificially low because they don't count **discouraged workers** (people who want a job but have not searched recently) and **underemployed workers** (people who are overqualified or working part-time but desiring full-time hours).

The number of working women is increasing. Like men, women work for personal satisfaction and to support themselves and their dependents. Based on motivation, there are four categories of working mothers: *captives* (would prefer to be full-time homemakers), *conflicted* (feel that their employment is harmful to their children), *copers* (have chosen jobs with enough flexibility to accommodate a family with a young child), and *committed* (have high occupational aspirations and a strong commitment to marriage and family). There are two variations on the traditional division of labor within marriage: the **two-person single career** (one spouse participates in the partner's career behind the scenes without pay or direct recognition) and ***stay at home dads*** (househusbands who stay at home to care for the family and do housework while their wives earn wages). There are several types of working families. These include: **dual-earner couples** (both partners work outside the home), **dual career couples** (both partners work in professional or managerial positions), **trailing spouses** (one partner gives up their work to search for another position in the location where a spouse has taken a job), and **commuter marriages** (married partners live and work in different geographic areas and get together intermittently). Couples vary in their **discretionary income** (the amount of money remaining after basic necessities have been paid). Almost 1/3 of women earn more than their husbands. If a husband holds traditional views about being the primary provider, an increasing salary gap tends to decrease his marital satisfaction while increasing his wife's marital satisfaction. There is little impact on marital power when wives earn more than their husbands. Couples typically ignore or minimize the income difference. When a couple violates traditional gender-role expectation, a process called *deviance neutralization* may take place in which husbands do less housework and wives do more. Work satisfaction and marital satisfaction have positive spillover effects in that one affects another. Women continue to perform more household work than men. Stress affects both mental and physical health. The most common sources of stress are money, work, and family related issues.

Women are more likely than men to encounter income discrimination, limited opportunities for advancement, and sexual harassment. There are two types of professional women: *career primary women* (sacrifice family and children for upward mobility and are groomed alongside ambitious men) and *career and family women* (allowed to work part-time and spend more time at home). The latter option is called the ***mommy track*** as it is a slower track or even a sidetrack for women who wanted to combine careers with childrearing. The **daddy penalty** is the phenomenon of penalizing the husbands of women who work outside the home. There is no place in the world where women's average wages equal those of men. This **wage gap**, or income difference, may result from sex discrimination in hiring, promotion, and pay; bias against mothers; and occupational segregation. Some women have tried to remedy the wage gap by filing individual or *class action suits* (legal proceedings that represent the interests of a larger group).The concept of **comparable worth** suggests that men and women should receive equal pay for doing similar work. Sexual harassment became illegal and a form of sex discrimination in 1964. It includes verbal behavior, nonverbal behavior, and physical contact.

The Pregnancy Discrimination Act of 1978 makes it illegal for employers with more than 15 workers to fire, demote, or penalize a pregnant employee. The 1993 Family and Medical Leave act allows eligible employees to take up to 12 weeks of unpaid, job protected, annual leave, with continuation of health benefits after the birth or adoption of a child, to care for a seriously sick family member, or to recover from their own illnesses. Many companies offer *flextime* (allowing workers to change their daily arrival and departure times) to accommodate parenting responsibilities. Sweden offers 15 months of paid leave to parents. Unlike other industrialized nations, the U.S. has no national child-care program. *Telecommuting* (working from home) is a flexible work style that allows parents to combine work and childrearing. The Personal Responsibility & Work Opportunity Reconciliation Act changed the welfare system by replacing AFDC with block grants.

PRE-TEST

1. The Chancellors are a homeless family. They live on the streets and they do not have food, clothes, or water. Because they lack the basic necessities of life, the Chancellors are experiencing:
   a. Absolute poverty
   b. Relative poverty
   c. Feminization of poverty

2. Hakim and Bianca are a married couple. They are both architects. Because both partners work in positions that require extensive training, a long-term commitment, and ongoing professional growth, Hakim and Bianca represent a:
   a. Dual earner couple
   b. Dual-career couple
   c. Two person single career couple

3. Bonita works as a truck driver for a furniture store. After learning that she was pregnant, the furniture delivery store fired Bonita. Bonita was reinstated when she reminded her boss that firing a woman because she is pregnant is illegal according to the:
   a. Pregnancy Discrimination Act of 1978
   b. Family and Medical Leave Act of 1993
   c. Both a & b

4. Bernard is a homeless beggar. Today, passers-by dropped a total of $21.00 into Bernard's outstretched hand. The $21 is Bernard's:
   a. Social class
   b. Wealth
   c. Income

5. BMW, a German company that assembles luxury cars in South Carolina, receives tax breaks from the state. This benefit provided by the state to a corporation is known as:
   a. Public assistance
   b. Corporate welfare
   c. AFDC

6. In a recent analysis of faculty pay at the local college, researchers found that those men who had employed wives received a lower salary than those men who had housewives. This illustrates:
   a. The mommy track
   b. The daddy penalty
   c. Comparable worth

7. Randy and Cherie rent a small apartment in a seedy neighborhood. They eat generic food and ride the bus to their jobs. When they compare themselves to other Americans, Randy and Cherie feel poor. This illustrates:
   a. Official poverty
   b. Absolute poverty
   c. Relative poverty

8. Grace is a single mother with 3 children. She works at a local packaging plant for minimum wage 50 weeks out of the year. Because Grace's income is below the poverty line for a family of four, Grace is a part of the:
   a. Absolute poor
   b. Working poor
   c. Relative poor

9. Monica sent her resume to over 300 companies and went on 63 interviews in the last 12 months. No one has offered her a job. Although Monica still wants a job, she has not sent her resume out because she feels that it is hopeless. Monica is a/an:
   a. Discouraged worker
   b. Underemployed worker
   c. Depressed worker

10. Sherry works part-time developing film at the local drug store. She would rather be working full time. As such, Sherry is a/an:
    a. Discouraged worker
    b. Underemployed worker
    c. Unemployed worker

11. Malawi is a widowed single-parent. She would rather be a full-time homemaker, but she has to work to provide for her family. Malawi's working mother role is:
    a. Conflicted
    b. Committed
    c. Captive

12. Samantha and Darren are a married couple. Darren is an ad executive and Samantha helps him with his ad campaigns by entertaining clients, editing his reports, and giving him feedback about his ideas. Because Samantha is helping with Darren's career behind the scenes, this reflects a:
    a. Two-person single career
    b. Trailing spouse
    c. Dual career couple

13. Lavonya is a teen parent. She does not have a high school diploma, job training, or work experience. Lavonya has a hard time finding a job because she lacks:
    a. Human capital
    b. Wealth
    c. Discretionary income

14. Marianne is a college professor. She teaches classes online and has enough flexibility to accommodate her family needs. Marianne's working mother role is:
    a. Conflicted
    b. Committed
    c. Coper

15. Rich and Beth are a married couple. He is a bartender and she is a waitress. Because both partners work outside the home, they are a:
    a. Dual career couple
    b. Dual earner couple
    c. Two-person single career couple

16. Women with children have an increasingly difficult time finding employment which is flexible enough to allow them to care for their children. Many women have to take low paying jobs. The growing number of poor women with children refers to:
    a. Relative poverty
    b. Absolute poverty
    c. The feminization of poverty

17. The Murdocks own a home that is worth $320,000, have a stock portfolio totaling $75,000 and have $28,000 in savings. These economic assets make up their:
    a. Wealth
    b. Income
    c. Social class

18. Tunga and Amina are a married couple. He is a college professor and she is an engineer in Pittsburgh, PA. When Tunga applies for and gets a job in New York City, Amina quits her job and looks for a job in New York City so that she can be with her husband. This illustrates the:
    a. Trailing spouse
    b. Two person single career couple
    c. Commuter marriage

19. Tang and Yi are a married couple. For the past 13 years, Tang has been the breadwinner and Yi has been the housewife. Now that Yi has a job, which is most likely to happen:
    a. Yi will do less housework
    b. Tang will do more housework
    c. Both a & b

20. Diane is a manager at a Fortune 500 Company. She was asked by her boss if she would like to decrease her hours to part-time so that she can spend more time at home with her family. Diane was very happy to reduce her work hours. Dianne is on the:
    a. Fast track
    b. Mommy track
    c. Family track

21. In Brazil, women earn 54% of what men earn. This illustrates:
    a. Discretionary income
    b. The wage gap
    c. Sexual harassment

22. Melanie is a news anchor. She just found out that she is pregnant. Although the network may be unhappy about her pregnancy, they cannot fire her. Pregnant women are protected from being fired or demoted by the:
    a. Pregnancy Discrimination Act of 1978
    b. Family and Medical Leave Act of 1993
    c. Both a & b

23. Edina works as a human resources manager in Baltimore, Maryland, and her husband Marvin works as a bailiff in a courtroom in Washington DC. The two rent separate apartments and come together every weekend. Edina and Marvin reflect the:
    a. Trailing spouse
    b. Commuter marriage
    c. Two person single career couple

24. When Charlene had a baby, her office allowed her to work from home through computer hookups to the company office. This illustrates:
    a. Flex-time
    b. Telecommuting
    c. Teleconferencing

25. Eileen and Maggie are liberal feminists who believe that men and women should receive equal pay for doing the same work. Eileen and Maggie believe in:
    a. The wage gap
    b. Discretionary income
    c. Comparable worth

EXERCISES/APPLICATIONS

1. Consider your favorite television family shows. Categorize the shows according to the type of working mother roles and the type of two-income family. Which styles are most prevalent? Which styles are least prevalent? What factors explain prevalence?

2. Outline the characteristics of your ideal marriage. What are the specific economic responsibilities of each partner? What are the specific childrearing responsibilities of each partner? What are the specific housework responsibilities of each person? What factors have shaped your ideas and how likely is it, in today's economy, for a couple to achieve your ideal?

CHAPTER 13 KEY TERMS CROSSWORD PUZZLE

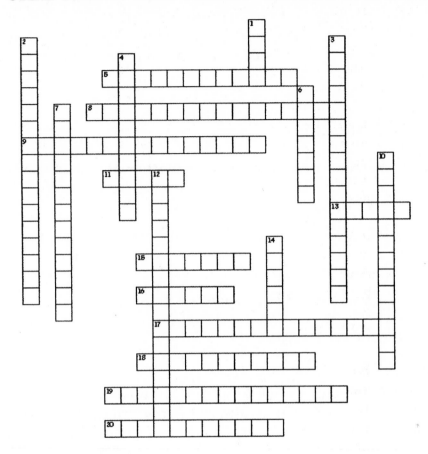

Across

5. He is the homemaker
8. Couple lives apart
9. Lacking basic necessities
11. Penalty his wife has a job
13. Working mom with flexible job
15. Unequal pay
16. Assets
17. Feeling poor
18. Minimum wage earners after 27 weeks of work
19. Equal pay for equal work
20. Minimum income set by the government

Down

1. Allows employees to take 12 weeks off
2. Government aid to businesses
3. Both partners work
4. Part time work for mother
6. Working mom who wants to be home
7. Income that is left over
10. Part-time worker who wants to be full-time
12. Two professional partners
14. Money received

POST-TEST

1. Rogelio is a janitor and Carmelita is a maid. They rent a small mobile home in the local trailer park. While they have the basic necessities to survive, this couple feels that they are poor compared to most Americans. This reflects:
   a. Absolute poverty
   b. Relative poverty
   c. Official poverty

2. Vilma is a college professor and the mother of a newborn baby. Vilma teaches all of her classes on-line, working from a home computer that is connected to her school. This illustrates:
   a. Telecommuting
   b. Teleconferencing
   c. Flex-time

3. In Norway, women earn 71% of what men earn. This illustrates:
   a. The wage gap
   b. Discretionary income
   c. Sexual harassment

4. Carla and Mike are a married couple. She is a book editor in New York City, and he is a dolphin trainer at Sea World in Orlando, Fl. The two get together at least twice each month. Carla and Mike reflect the:
   a. Trailing spouse
   b. Commuter marriage
   c. Two person single career couple

5. Tim founded his company on the belief that men and women should receive equal pay for doing the same work. Tim believes in:
   a. The wage gap
   b. Discretionary income
   c. Comparable worth

6. Samba and Duk are a married couple. They are both physicians. Because both partners work in positions that require extensive training, a long-term commitment, and ongoing professional growth, Samba and Duk represent a:
   a. Dual-career couple
   b. Dual earner couple
   c. Two person single career couple.

7. As a housewife, Mrs. Mills depended on her husband to care for her and the children. After the divorce, she got custody of the kids and her household income dropped by 80%. Mrs. Mills found herself in poverty. This growing number of poor women and children refers to:
   a. Absolute poverty
   b. Relative poverty
   c. Feminization of poverty

8. After paying for rent, car insurance, utilities, child care, and food, the Ricardo family has $200 left each month. This $200 is an example of:
   a. Income
   b. Wealth
   c. Discretionary income

9. Tyson is a school teacher. He works from August to May and has the summer to spend with his 4 children. Since his wife died, Tyson's family income falls below the official poverty level. This school teacher is a part of the:
   a. Working poor
   b. Relative poor
   c. Absolute poor

10. Chuck and Barbara Peek are a married couple. Chuck is a professor at the local university. Barbara supports Chuck's career by entertaining faculty and students, doing library research, typing his articles, and grading his exams. This reflects a:
    a. Two-person single career
    b. Trailing spouse
    c. Dual career couple

11. Claudette is a junior partner in a law firm, and she has 3 children. Claudette is working to be partner in the firm, and she also wants to be a great wife and mother. Claudette's working mother role is:
    a. Conflicted
    b. Committed
    c. Captive

12. Tiana is a sales manager with 2 children. Tiana believes that her employment negatively effects her children, and she is working extra hard to save enough money so that she can stay at home with her children until they are school-aged. Tiana's working mother role is:
    a. Conflicted
    b. Captive
    c. Coper

13. Lisette has a doctoral degree in forensic psychology. She would like to work for one of the local criminal justice entities. Until she can land her dream job, she is working as a nanny for her neighbors. Lisette is a/an
    a. Discouraged worker
    b. Unemployed worker
    c. Underemployed worker

14. Roseanne and Dan are a married couple. Dan is a construction worker, and Roseanne works at the local plant. Because both partners work outside the home, they are a:
    a. Dual career couple
    b. Dual earner couple
    c. Two-person single career couple

15. Fisher graduated with his bachelor's degree and worked for 2 years as an intern for an ad executive. Fisher's education, work experience, and specialized skills illustrate the concept of:
    a. Wealth
    b. Discretionary income
    c. Human capital

16. Which of the following is determined by multiplying 3 times the annual cost of a minimum nutrient food budget?
    a. Absolute poverty
    b. Poverty line
    c. Relative poverty

17. The state of Maryland provided a corporation with grant money to pay monthly rent. The benefits provided by the state to assist a corporation is called:
    a. Corporate welfare
    b. AFDC
    c. Public assistance

18. Tiffany is a hairstylist. She makes $3,000 per week styling hair and she receives another $2,000 per month in alimony from her ex-husband. This money that Tiffany receives is:
    a. Income
    b. Wealth
    c. Social class

19. When they married, Bill and Frenchie had $700 in the bank and a beat up Volkswagon worth $150. These assets refer to Bill and Frenchie's:
    a. Social class
    b. Income
    c. Wealth

20. It is going to be a harsh winter for the Sadler family. They do not have the food, clothes, or shelter that they need to survive. This family is experiencing:
    a. Feminization of poverty
    b. Absolute poverty
    c. Relative poverty

21. After 30 years, Martin retired from his family's law firm and married a woman 20 years younger than he. Martin and his new wife have 2 young children. While Martin's wife works as a dentist, he stays home to care for the family and do the housework. Martin is a:
    a. Trailing spouse
    b. Househusband
    c. Discouraged worker

22. George argues that as long as society has poor people, there will be someone to work in the most undesirable jobs, like coal mines. George believes that poverty serves:
    a. Functions
    b. Dysfunctions
    c. None of the above

23. Nadia works as a security guard at a bank. After learning that Nadia is pregnant, the bank fired Nadia. Nadia wants to know if she has any protection under the law to secure her position as a security guard. Nadia should read about the:
    a. Pregnancy Discrimination Act of 1978
    b. Family and Medical Leave Act of 1993
    c. Both a & b

24. When Onay had surgery, she had to miss work for 7 months. Although Onay did not get paid while she was out, her employers had to hold her job for her. This right is granted to workers through the:
    a. Pregnancy Discrimination Act of 1978
    b. Family and Medical Leave Act of 1993
    c. Both a & b

25. Ross and Phoebe are having a debate. Both of them are underemployed and each thinks that they would be better off if they were of the opposite sex. Which of the following is true?
   a. Men are more likely than women to suffer from underemployment.
   b. Women are more likely than men to suffer from underemployment.
   c. Men and women are equally likely to suffer from underemployment

SELF-ASSESSMENT:
HOW RICH ARE YOU IN HUMAN CAPITAL?

Directions: Read each statement. Put a check in the box to reflect whether or not it is true.

	True	False
I have a high school diploma or its equivalent.		
I am pursuing a college degree.		
I have good writing skills.		
I have a trade school certificate.		
I have a college degree.		
I have taken non-credit courses.		
I have work experience.		
I work well with others.		
I am good at math.		
I have a solid professional network.		
I can type.		
I am articulate.		
I exercise to maintain my health.		
I am good at problem solving.		
I eat nutritiously to maintain my health.		
I have work experience in at least two areas.		
I am able to obtain positive letters of recommendation.		
I have experience in leadership.		
I have computer skills.		
I am an overachiever.		

Key: Give yourself 1 point for every statement that you checked as 'True.' A score of 20 represents the person with the most human capital. A score of 0 represents the person with the least human capital and suggests lots of room for improvement.

ANSWERS

PRE-TEST

Answers	Page Numbers
1. A	389
2. B	401
3. A	413
4. A	386
5. C	389
6. B	408
7. C	389
8. B	392
9. A	396
10. B	396
11. C	398
12. A	399
13. A	391
14. C	398
15. B	401
16. C	391
17. A	386
18. A	402
19. C	404
20. B	407
21. B	408
22. A	413
23. B	403
24. B	415
25. C	409

KEY TERMS CROSSWORD PUZZLE

Across	Page Numbers
5. Househusband	400
8. Commuter Marriage	403
9. Absolute Poverty	389
11. Daddy	408
13. Coper	398
15. Wage Gap	408
16. Wealth	386
17. Relative Poverty	389
18. Working Poor	392
19. Comparable worth	409
20. Poverty line	390

Down	
1. FMLA	413
2. Corporate welfare	389
3. Dual earner couple	401
4. Mommy track	407
6. Captive	398

POST-TEST

Answers		Page Numbers
1.	B	389
2.	A	416
3.	A	408
4.	B	403
5.	C	409
6.	A	401
7.	C	391
8.	C	401
9.	A	392
10.	A	399
11.	B	398
12.	A	398
13.	C	396
14.	B	401
15.	C	391
16.	B	390
17.	A	389
18.	A	386
19.	C	386
20.	B	389
21.	B	400
22.	A	392
23.	A	413
24.	B	413
25.	B	396

FAMILY VIOLENCE AND OTHER HEALTH ISSUES

CHAPTER OBJECTIVES

Upon reading Chapter Fourteen, students should be able to:

1.   Explain the types, prevalence, and predictors of marital and intimate partner violence.

2.   Describe the three phases of the cycle of domestic violence.

3.   Explain the reasons why women remain in abusive situations.

4.   Discuss the issues surrounding the abuse of men by women.

5.   Explain the types, prevalence, and predictors of child maltreatment.

6.   Explain the types, prevalence, and predictors of sibling abuse.

7.   Explain the types, prevalence, and predictors of adolescent abuse.

8.   Explain the types, prevalence, and predictors of elder abuse.

9.   Discuss violence among same-sex couples.

10.   Discuss violence among racial-ethnic immigrants.

11.   Explain the theories of violence.

12.   Discuss drug abuse and how it impacts family life.

13.   Discuss depression and suicide and how they impact family life.

14.   Discuss eating disorders and how they impact family life.

15.   Describe the methods used to combat domestic violence and other crisis.

CHAPTER OVERVIEW

Intimate partner violence may be either *physical* (includes throwing objects, pushing, grabbing, shoving, slapping, kicking, biting, hitting, beating, choking, threatening with a knife or gun, and using a knife or gun), *sexual* (a person is forced to have sexual intercourse or take part in an unwanted sexual activity), or *emotional* (psychological and emotional). Women are more likely than men to experience violence by an intimate partner. Men are more likely than women to engage in repeated violence against their partners. When couples have *status compatibility*, they are fairly similar on variables like education, income, and economic contributions. In *status reversal*, women are higher than men on such measures. Status reversal increases the likelihood that a woman will experience partner violence. **Marital rape** (an abusive act in which a man forces his wife to have unwanted sex) has been a crime in all states since 1993. However, 30 states grant a *marital rape exemption* (prosecution is suspended). Some imprisoned women have been pardoned by their respective governors for killing or assaulting partners who had physically abused them. These women give a defense based on the **battered-woman syndrome**, a condition that describes a woman who has experienced many years of physical abuse and who feels incapable of leaving.   The "cycle theory of battering incidents" suggests that there is a three-phase cycle involved in marital abuse, beginning with the *tension-building* phase (wife tries to prevent her husband's anger from escalating), leading to the *acute battering incident* (husband explodes into a rage of abusing his wife), and ending with the *calm* or *honeymoon* phase (husband begs for forgiveness, makes promises, and wife accepts). This cycle repeats. There are several reasons why women stay in abusive relationships: negative self-concept, a belief that the abuser will change, economic hardship, the need for child support, sense of shame or guilt, self-blame, fear, and a prison-like home.

Child maltreatment includes a broad range of behaviors that place a child at serious risk or result in serious harm. *Physical abuse* causes bodily injury to a child. *Munchausen syndrome by proxy* occurs when an adult feigns or induces a child's illness to attract medical attention. *Sexual abuse* involves the child in sexual activity. *Neglect* is the caregiver's failure to provide the child with basic necessities. There are different types of neglect: *medical neglect* (failure to provide the appropriate health care), *stimulation neglect* (failure to engage in activities that nourish the child's cognitive development), and *language neglect* (failure to develop the child's communication skills). *Emotional abuse* conveys to a child that they are inferior, worthless, flawed, unloved, or unwanted. This may include *spurning* (threatening to hurt, kill, or abandon a child), *isolating* (denying a child opportunities to interact with others), or *corrupting* (being a poor role model and permitting or encouraging a child's antisocial behaviors). *Incest* is sexual intercourse between close blood relatives. Abused children are more likely to have parents who: abuse drugs and alcohol, are experiencing economic stress and poverty, are engaged in partner violence, and have been divorced.

There are various forms of sibling abuse, including name-calling and ridicule, degradation, promoting fear, torturing or killing a pet, destroying personal possessions, and sexual abuse. About 10% of all murders in families are *siblicide* (killing one's sibling). Although family violence decreases as children get older, a large number of parents abuse teenagers. Baby boomers, now in their early forties to late fifties, are often referred to as the **sandwich generation** because they care for their own children and their aging parents. Elder abuse includes physical abuse, negligence, financial exploitation, psychological abuse, deprivation of basic needs, isolation from friends and family, and failure to administer needed medications. Adult children are the largest group of elder abusers, followed by the victim's spouse. Risk factors for elder abuse include shared living arrangement, social isolation, alcohol abuse, impairments, dependency, medical costs, stress, negative personality characteristics, and the intergenerational transmission of violence. In gay and lesbian households, researchers estimate that the incidence of battering between couples is about the same as it is for heterosexual couples, and much of the abuse is recurrent. Immigrant women typically experience more domestic violence than their American-born counterparts. Recent immigrants rarely report abuse.

Patriarchy/male-dominance theory maintains that men's domestic violence is created and condoned by men's authority. *Social-learning theory* posits that aggression and violence are learned by observing others. *Resource theory* suggests that men with the fewest resources are the most likely to resort to violence. *Exchange theory* argues that victimizers and victims tolerate or engage in violent behavior because it offers more benefits than costs. *Ecological systems theory* explains domestic violence through an analysis of relationships between individuals and larger systems.

Many families have to deal with drug abuse, use of **steroids** (synthetic hormones used to improve sports performance), **depression** (pervasive sadness), suicide, **anorexia nervosa** (eating disorder involving fear of obesity, distorted body image and belief that one is fat) and **bulimia** (eating disorder involving a pattern of eating binges followed by vomiting, fasting, excessive exercise, or the use of diuretics and laxatives). Efforts to raise public awareness about domestic violence may help in the prevention and intervention of maltreatment and family crises.

PRE-TEST

1. Cliff is an obstetrician. Clair is a lawyer. They both have post graduate degrees and they both contribute equal amounts to the monthly household budget. This couple is experiencing:
   a) Status compatibility
   b) Status reversal
   c) Both a &b

2. After getting drunk, Tony Montana forced his wife Elvira to have sex with him. This illustrates:
   a) Marital rape exemption
   b) Siblicide
   c) Marital rape

3. Monroe and his wife Theresa have been caught in the cycle of battering incidents. Last night, Monroe broke Theresa's ribs. Which phase does this represent?
   a) Tension-building
   b) Acute battering
   c) Calm

4. Erin is a diabetic 7 year old. She needs insulin everyday. Her mother is so concerned with her own problems that she fails to ensure that Erin has her insulin. Erin gets sick. This is an example of:
   a) Medical neglect
   b) Munchausen syndrome by proxy
   c) Both a & b

5. Jack and Jill are debating about the prevalence of sexual abuse. Jack believes that sexual abuse of children is more likely to involve uncles. Jill believes that it is more likely to involve fathers. Which is true?
   a) Most cases of reported incest involves fathers
   b) Most cases of reported incest involves uncles
   c) Fathers and uncles are equally likely to sexually abuse

6. Pedro will present a paper on the most common form of emotional abuse among siblings. Pedro's paper will cover:
   a) Degradation
   b) Name calling

c) Promoting fear

7. Keri is a paralegal and Doug is a delivery driver. Kerri earns more than her husband Doug and contributes a larger share to the household budget. This couple is experiencing:
a) Status compatibility
b) Status reversal
c) Both a &b

8. Ade and Fatima are baby boomers who take care of their children and their parents. Ade and Fatima are a part of the:
a) Boomerang generation
b) Caretaking generation
c) Sandwich generation

9. Vincent and Lawrence are having a debate. Vincent believes that homosexual couples experience more domestic violence than heterosexual couples. Lawrence believes that heterosexual couples experience more domestic violence. What should they know?
a) The prevalence of battering is greater in heterosexual couples
b) The prevalence of battering is greater in homosexual couples
c) The prevalence of violence is about the same in heterosexual and homosexual couples.

10. In Iraq, men have more power, status, and privilege than women. Violence against women is common because the men's authority condones domestic violence. Which theory supports this assertion?
a) Patriarchy
b) Resources
c) Social learning

11. Mr. Bunker always disciplined his children with spankings and chastised his wife with slaps across the face. Little Archie grew up in this violent household and observed that abusive behavior was the way to resolve conflicts. Now that Little Archie is an adult, he spanks his children and slaps his wife. The theory that best explains this is:
a) Resources
b) Social learning
c) Ecological

12. Marino is an unemployed bartender. His wife has more money, more education, and a more prestigious job. Juan is an employed bartender. He has more money and more education than his homemaker wife. Resources theory suggests that:
a) Marino is more likely to abuse his wife
b) Juan is more likely to abuse his wife

c) Juan and Marino are equally likely to abuse their wives

13. Mona called the police to report that her husband forced her to have sex against her will. However, because she and her husband live together, the case was not prosecuted. This reflects:
a) Emotional abuse
b) The marital rape exemption
c) Siblicide

14. Stacy injected her daughter with urine so that her daughter would get an infection. Then Stacy rushed her daughter to the hospital for medical care. Stacy thrives off of sympathy and attention. This represents which form of child maltreatment?
a) Medical neglect
b) Munchausen syndrome by proxy
c) Both a & b

15. Research suggests that elder abuse is much higher when there is a combination of macro and micro variables. Which theory supports this assertion that one must consider the individual and the larger social systems?
a) Patriarchy
b) Ecological
c) Social learning

16. Sonia is concerned about her son. He wants to get a scholarship to the local university, and he has said that he would do anything to get in. Sonia is worried that her son will take synthetic hormones or _____ to improve his athletic skills.
a) Pheromones
b) Laxatives
c) Steroids

17. Amanda has to do an in-class presentation on suicide. She will report that among adults, _____ are most likely to commit suicide.
a) White men
b) White women
c) Black men

18. Sasha has a severe fear of obesity and believes that she is fat. She has experienced significant weight loss as a result of which eating disorder?
a) Bulimia
b) Munchausen syndrome by proxy
c) Anorexia nervosa

19. Quincy forced his younger sister to engage in sexual intercourse with him. This is called:
a) Incest
b) Sexual abuse
c) Both a & b

20. On Saturday, Lonnie stayed up all night binging on Oreo cookies. On Sunday morning, she induced herself to vomit and took several laxatives. She does not plan to eat again until Wednesday. Lonnie suffers from which eating disorder?
a) Bulimia
b) Munchausen syndrome by proxy
c) Anorexia nervosa

21. Renee is presenting an in-class report on age and violence in intimate relationships. Renee reports that:
a) Younger people are more likely than older people to be involved in domestic violence
b) Older people are more likely than younger people to be involved in domestic violence
c) Younger and older people are equally likely to be involved in domestic violence

22. Karen has been physically abused by her husband for 17 years. She feels trapped and does not believe that she has what it would take to leave her husband. Karen suffers from:
a) Munchausen syndrome by proxy
b) Battered woman syndrome
c) Sandwich generation

23. Sean's parents do not talk to him at all. He fails to develop communication skills, and at the age of 5, he has the verbal abilities. of an 18 month old. This reflects:
a) Emotional abuse
b) Language neglect
c) Physical abuse

24. Pia asked her teacher if mothers or fathers are more likely to abuse their children. The teacher correctly replied:
a) Mothers
b) Fathers
c) They are equally likely

25. Phillip killed his two sisters. This is an example of:
   a) Suicide
   b) Patricide
   c) Siblicide

EXERCISES/APPLICATIONS

1.   In the United States, some states grant a *marital-rape exemption.* Which macro and micro-level social forces have led to the adoption of such an escape clause? Do you support or oppose the exemption? Why or why not?

2.   Consider contemporary music. Which, if any, types of domestic violence have you heard depicted in the lyrics of songs? Have you seen any domestic violence depicted in music videos? Do you think that such depictions contribute to domestic violence?

CHAPTER 14 KEY TERMS CROSSWORD PUZZLE

Across

2. Threatening to hurt or kill child
3. Husband forces wife to have sex
7. Mistreating senior citizens
10. Sex between close relatives
11. Killing brothers or sisters
12. Phase where abuser is sorry
13. When she makes more money than him
14. Generation caring for parents & children

Down

1. Synthetic hormones
4. Theory suggesting that male authority leads to violence
5. Pervasive sadness
6. Involves fear of obesity
8. Involves eating binges
9. To tell kids that they are worthless

POST-TEST

1. Mrs. Winsky is on trial for killing her husband. Mr. Winsky had physically abused his wife for 32 years and she felt incapable of leaving him. One day, when he tried to kick her, she stabbed and killed him. Mrs. Winsky suffers from:
   a. Battered woman syndrome
   b. Anorexia Nervosa
   c. Munchausen syndrome by proxy

2. DeAndre forced his daughter to engage in sexual intercourse with him. This is called:
   a. Incest
   b. Sexual abuse
   c. Both a & b

3. Each week, Lynn's softball team goes out for pizza after the game. Lynn eats more food than any of her teammates. Once she goes home, she induces herself to vomit and takes several laxatives. She will not eat again for a few days. Lynn suffers from which eating disorder?
   a. Bulimia
   b. Munchausen syndrome by proxy
   c. Anorexia nervosa

4. Elsa is presenting an in-class report on social class and violence in intimate relationships. Elsa reports that:
   a. Lower income people are more likely than higher income people to be involved in domestic violence
   b. Higher income people are more likely than lower income people to be involved in domestic violence
   c. Lower income people and higher income people are equally likely to be involved in domestic violence

5. Ramona is a teenager who is concerned about how she looks. Ramona wanted to lose weight so that she could more closely resemble the supermodels in her favorite magazines. Ramona took some synthetic hormones or:
   a. Pheromones
   b. Laxatives
   c. Steroids

6. Beatriz is a college-educated bank manager. Her cousin, Laila is an unemployed single parent who dropped out of high school. According to resource theory, which woman is more likely to date an abusive man?
   a. Laila
   b. Beatriz
   c. They are equally likely

7. Tammy's parents always punched her when she misbehaved. She thought that it was for her own good. Now that Tammy is a parent, she punches her children when they misbehave. This is explained by which theory?
   a. Resources
   b. Social learning
   c. Patriarchy

8. In America, men have more power, status, and prestige. The authority that men have has created an atmosphere that condones domestic violence against women. Which theory is supported by this idea?
   a. Resources
   b. Social learning
   c. Patriarchy

9. When Malcolm was growing up, his parents physically abused him. Now, Malcolm is caring for his elderly parents, and he physically abuses them. This pattern is called:
   a. The cycle of retaliation
   b. The cycle of violence
   c. Violent family life course development

10. Olivia is an 87 year old woman. She can no longer live on her own and must go and live with either her son or her daughter. Olivia wants to live with the child who is least likely to abuse her. What should Olivia know?
    a. Men are more likely than women to engage in elder abuse
    b. Women are more likely than men to engage in elder abuse
    c. Men and women are equally likely to engage in elder abuse

11. Dukin and Alaria take care of their children and their parents. There are currently 3 generations living in their household. Dukin and Alaria are a part of the:
    a. Boomerang generation
    b. Sandwich generation
    c. Caretaking generation

12. Katrina and Josh lock their 7 year old daughter in a closet every day when she comes home from school. She is not allowed to interact with others. This is an example of which form of emotional abuse?
    a. Isolating
    b. Terrorizing
    c. Corrupting

13. The Washingtons believe that it is acceptable for their eight year old son to visit violent pornographic web sites. They say "boys will be boys." Permitting this inappropriate behavior is an example of:
    a. Corrupting
    b. Terrorizing
    c. Isolating

14. Antoinette is a drug addict. In order to purchase drugs, she sells her 9 year old daughter for sexual favors. This is an example of:
    a. Sexual abuse
    b. Physical abuse
    c. Emotional abuse

15. Elaine suffocated her son to the point of unconsciousness and then rushed him to the hospital to get medical attention. Elaine desires sympathy and attention. This represents which form of child maltreatment?
    a. Medical neglect
    b. Munchausen syndrome by proxy
    c. Both a & b

16. Lillith is in the hospital with internal injuries because her husband kicked her with his steel-toed boots. Her husband visits her in the hospital and brings flowers and candy. He begs Lillith to forgive him and promises that he will never hurt her again. This phase is known as the:
    a. Tension-building
    b. Acute battering
    c. Calm

17. Vertigo tells his wife Bea that she is ugly, fat, and dumb. This illustrates:
    a. Emotional abuse
    b. Verbal abuse
    c. Both a & b

18. Maggie was not feeling well, and she took a few sedatives and went to bed. Her husband got in the bed with her and tried to initiate sex. When Maggie refused, her husband forced her to have sex with him. This illustrates:
    a. Siblicide
    b. Marital rape
    c. Marital rape exemption

19. Monica is a five star chef, and her husband Chandler is unemployed and looking for a job as a waiter. Monica has a higher social status than her husband and is supporting the household with her pay check and savings. This couple is experiencing:
    a. Status compatibility
    b. Status reversal
    c. Both a &b

20. Tedra is a Family Services Worker for the Department of Children & Families. Tedra's job is to respond to reports of a broad range of behaviors that put children at risk. Tedra's job deals with:
    a. Elder abuse
    b. Child maltreatment
    c. Both a & b

21. Sandra and Elvin both graduated from Princeton with their graduate degrees. They both work in professional positions, and they make equal contributions to the household income. This couple is experiencing:
    a. Status compatibility
    b. Status reversal
    c. Both a & b

22. Eduardo argues that families are safe havens. Adina argues that families are dangerous pits. Which of the following is true?
    a. People are more likely to be killed by a family member than a stranger
    b. People are more likely to be killed by a stranger than a family member
    c. People are equally likely to be killed by a family member and a stranger

23. Veronica and Gwendolyn want to know if there is a relationship between marital status and domestic violence. The fact is that:
    a. Married women experience the highest rates of domestic violence
    b. Divorced women experience the highest rates of domestic violence
    c. Separated women experience the highest rates of domestic violence

24. Justin needs to have his asthma pump with him to ward off asthma attacks. His mother does not provide a pump for him. She uses the money for the pump to purchase alcohol and drugs. Justin has an asthma attack and is hospitalized. His mother is guilty of:
    a. Emotional abuse
    b. Munchausen syndrome by proxy
    c. Medical neglect

25. Valerie reported that her husband raped her, but her husband was never prosecuted because of a loophole that prohibits a man from being prosecuted for raping his wife if they live together. This loophole is called the:
    a. Marital rape exemption
    b. Husband's rights clause
    c. Both a & b

SELF-ASSESSMENT:
HOW ABUSIVE WAS YOUR SIBLING?

Directions: Read each statement. Put a check in the box to reflect whether or not the statement is true or false.

	True	False
My sibling slapped me.		
My sibling punched me.		
My sibling kicked me.		
My sibling called me names.		
My sibling made fun of me.		
My sibling made me feel worthless.		
My sibling instilled fear in me.		
My sibling mistreated my pet.		
My sibling killed my pet.		
My sibling touched me in a sexual manner.		
My sibling forced me to engage in sexual behaviors.		
My sibling hid my personal possessions.		
My sibling destroyed my personal possessions.		
My sibling used a weapon against me.		
My sibling told lies to me.		

Key: Give yourself 1 point for every statement that you checked as 'True.' A score of 15 represents the person who had a very abusive sibling. A score of 0 represents the person who had a non-abusive sibling.

ANSWERS

PRE-TEST

Answers	Page Numbers
1. A	424
2. C	425
3. B	425
4. A	430
5. A	434
6. B	434
7. B	424
8. C	438
9. C	441
10. A	442
11. B	442
12. A	442
13. B	425
14. B	430
15. B	444
16. C	445
17. A	447
18. C	468
19. C	430
20. A	448
21. A	423
22. B	425
23. B	430
24. A	432
25. C	437

KEY TERMS CROSSWORD PUZZLE

Across	Page Numbers
2. Terrorizing	430
3. Marital rape	425
7. Elder abuse	439
10. Incest	434
11. Siblicide	437
12. Honeymoon	425
13. Status reversal	436
14. Sandwich	438

Down	
1. Steroids	445
4. Patriarchy	442
5. Depression	446
6. Anorexia Nervosa	448
8. Bulimia	448
9. Emotional abuse	422

POST-TEST

Answers	Page Numbers
1. A	425
2. C	430
3. A	448
4. A	423
5. C	445
6. A	442
7. B	442
8. C	442
9. B	441
10. A	429
11. B	438
12. A	430
13. A	430
14. A	430
15. B	430
16. C	425
17. A	430
18. B	425
19. B	424
20. B	429
21. A	424
22. A	432
23. C	423
24. C	430
25. A	425

SEPARATION AND DIVORCE

15

CHAPTER OBJECTIVES

Upon reading Chapter Fifteen, students should be able to:

1.   Explain the process and outcomes of separation.

2.   Discuss divorce trends in the U.S. and around the globe.

3.   Describe the six stations of divorce.

4.   Compare and contrast ways that divorced parents relate to one another.

5.   Explain why people divorce.

6.   Discuss the consequences of divorce for adults.

7.   Compare and contrast the different types of custody.

8.   Discuss trends in child support.

9.   Explain how divorce impacts children.

10.   Compare and contrast divorce intervention strategies.

CHAPTER OVERVIEW

Separation is a period in which married couples live apart and involves four phases: *preseparation* (partners physically separate after experiencing emotional alienation), *early separation* (partners try to find answers to their questions), *midseparation* (partners face the realities of everyday life), and *late separation* (partners learn how to survive as singles again). About 10% percent of all married U.S. couples who have separated have reconciled. Older women are more likely than younger women to reconcile. **Divorce** is the legal and formal dissolution of a marriage. Divorce rates around the globe are rising. Women are more likely than men to seek divorce in all countries. There are six stations of divorce: *emotional divorce* (one partner detaches emotionally), *legal divorce* (formal dissolution of the marriage), *economic divorce* (partners argue about money and property), *coparental divorce* (partners make agreements about responsibilities for the children), *community divorce* (partners inform others that they are no longer married and some relationships change), and *psychic* divorce (partners establish separate lives). **Alimony** (spousal maintenance) and **child support** (monetary payments by the non-custodial parent to the custodial parent to help pay child-rearing expenses) are decided upon during the legal divorce. Divorced parents may relate to one another as *perfect pals* (share decision making and child-rearing as they did when they were married), *cooperative colleagues* (negotiate and compromise to minimize the trauma of divorce for children), *angry associates* (harbor bitter resentments and have heated battles), *fiery foes* (completely unable to co-parent), and *dissolved duos* (break with each other entirely).

Macro-level factors that influence divorce include new social institutions (all states have **no-fault divorce** laws so that neither partner needs to establish the guilt of the other), weakened **social integration** (the social bonds that people have with others and the community at large), changing gender roles, more individualistic cultural values, and technological advances. Demographic risk factors for divorce include parental divorce, early age at marriage, premarital childbearing, teens in the home, being African American, low education, and low income. Interpersonal risk factors for divorce include unrealistic expectations, conflict and abuse, infidelity, and communication problems. Divorced people report greater social isolation, economic hardship, and economic stress. The *divorce hangover* occurs when a divorced person is unable to let go, develop new friendships, and reorient themselves as single.

Custody is a court mandated ruling as to which parent will have primary responsibility for the welfare and upbringing of a couple's children. Children live with the custodial parent and see the non-custodial parent according to specific visitation schedules. There are three types of custody: **sole custody** (one parent has sole responsibility for raising the child), **split custody** (children are divided between the parents by gender or choice), and **joint custody** (children divide their time between both parents who share in decision-making and upbringing). There are two types of joint custody: *joint legal* (parents share decision making on important issues) and *joint physical* (courts decide how much time children will spend in each parent's home). **Co-custody** is a new term used when parents share physical and legal custody equally. Laws on custody among gay parents vary from one state to another. **Child abduction** is the taking or keeping of a child by a family member in violation of a custody order, decree, or other custodial right.

Nearly half of all men neither see nor support their children after divorce. Non-custodial parents are more likely to pay full or partial child support payments when they have joint custody and visitation rights. Nonpaying fathers fall into four categories: *parent in pain* (feels shut out from the family and distances himself from the children), *overextended parent* (overburdened with financial obligations), *vengeful parent* (uses child support as a mean of control), and *irresponsible parent* (simply does not take his parental duties seriously). In 1984, Congress passed the Child Support Enforcement Amendment that requires states to deduct delinquent support from delinquent parents' paychecks and tax returns. The Family Support Act of 1988 mandates periodic reviews of award levels to keep up with the rate of inflation. The Deadbeat Parents Act of 1998 makes it a felony for anyone who crosses a state line to evade child support obligations.

There are five types of divorce that impact children into adulthood. The *disappearing parent* leaves the home suddenly with no explanation. Children grew up to be suspicious. In the *surprise divorce*, parents often seemed close but one filed for divorce without warning. Children grow up to avoid intimate relationships because they expect partners to be undependable. The *violent divorce* involves spousal and sometimes child abuse. The children grow up to repress conflict for fear of violence or to believe that conflict is a way to test intimacy. The *late divorce* involves parents staying together for the kids' sake. Children may grow up to equate love with suffering in silence or to believe that good relationships are impossible. The *protect-the-kids divorce*, parents decide to protect their children by withholding information about the real reasons for the divorce. Some stressors that decrease children's development and adjustment to divorce are long term parental problems, poor parenting, parental conflict and hostility, and economic hardship and negative outcomes over the life course. The intergenerational transmission of divorce refers to the negative consequences of divorce that impact the 2nd and 3rd generation. Children who experience the least negative effects are those who get support from friends, neighbors, and schools. The major positive outcome of divorce is that it provides options to people in unsatisfactory marriages. Additionally, parental separation is better for children than remaining in an intact family where there is continuous conflict.

Counseling and marital therapy can help married and divorcing parents build stronger relationships with each other and their children. **Divorce mediation** is a technique and practice in which a trained arbitrator helps the divorcing couple to come to an agreement. Mediation increases communication, reduces conflict, creates a more cooperative attitude, makes it easier to accommodate changes as children grow, and prevents children from being pawns.

PRE-TEST

1. Phillip and Vivian are the divorced parents of four children. After the divorce, Vivian left town with the children and Phillip has not seen or heard from them since then. He has no idea where they are or if they are dead or alive. Phillip and Vivian are:
   a. Fiery foes
   b. Angry associates
   c. Dissolved duos

2. When Brad and Ashley were married, Brad played golf with his father-in-law, John, once a week. Now that Ashley and Brad are divorced, Brad and John have severed their relationship. This reflects which station of divorce?
   a. Community
   b. Psychic
   c. Emotional

3. Mike and Carol Brady have three sons and three daughters. When they divorced, the boys went with Mike, and the girls stayed with Carol. This reflects which custody arrangement?
   a. Joint custody
   b. Sole custody
   c. Split custody

4. After separating for a while, both Mork and Mindy felt a sense of guilt over abandoning the marriage, and they reunited in a "pseudo-reconciliation" which did not last long. Mork and Mindy were in which stage of separation:
   a. Early separation
   b. Mid-separation
   c. Late separation

5. Tommy and Pam are the divorced parents of two. The court has ordered Tommy to pay child support. However, Tommy wants to punish Pam, so he does not. Tommy represents the:
   a. Parent in pain
   b. Overloaded parent
   c. Vengeful parent

6. Tom and Helen Willis are getting a divorce. The judge has ordered Mr. Willis to provide his wife with a spousal maintenance payment of $12,000 per month. This is known as:
   a. Child support
   b. Alimony
   c. Both a & b

7. Today, Stanley and Helen Roper went to court to dissolve their marital ties. The couple is in which station of divorce?
   a. Legal
   b. Co-parental
   c. Economic

8. Tony and Angela are talking about the chances of a separated couple reconciling. Angela believes that most separated couples reconcile. Tony believes that most do not. The fact is:
   a. Most separated couples reconcile
   b. Most separated couples do not reconcile
   c. There is no data on the reconciliation of separated couples

9. Lynn and Andy are divorced, and Andy has custody of Opie, their son. As the non-custodial parent, Lynn is expected to make monetary payments to Andy to help with Opie's expenses. Lynn is expected to pay:
   a. Alimony
   b. Child support
   c. Both a & b

10. Frasier and Lillith divorced last year. This year, their son Frederick wants to go to space camp. Frasier and Lillith argue over who should cover these extra expenses. They are in which station of divorce?
    a. Community
    b. Psychic
    c. Economic

11. Florida and James are the divorced parents of three children. The ex-spouses still spend the holidays together and maintain contact with each other's extended family. They represent:
    a. Cooperative colleagues
    b. Dissolved duos
    c. Perfect pals

12. Two years after the divorce, Jill reclaimed her maiden name to symbolize that she was finally establishing a life that was separate from her ex-husband's. This reflects which station of divorce:
    a. Emotional
    b. Psychic
    c. Community

13. Bobby and Whitney are divorcing. Nether of them have to establish guilt or wrongdoing on the part of the other. They simply report that they are ending the marriage for irreconcilable differences. They are able to do this because of:
    a. No-fault divorce
    b. Decreased social integration
    c. Changing gender roles

14. Monica and Chandler live in a tight-knit community. There are lots of opportunities for people to connect to one another. Their community has a high level of:
    a. Cultural values
    b. Social integration
    c. Technology

15. Sheila and Eric are divorced, but Sheila refuses to let go. She will not develop new social ties and she hopes that they can reconcile. Sheila is experiencing:
    a. Separation anxiety
    b. Psychic divorce
    c. Divorce hangover

16. Lenny and Laverne are divorced. The judge ordered that Laverne has full responsibility for raising the child and that Lenny has some visitation rights. This reflects which custody arrangement?
    a. Split custody
    b. Joint custody
    c. Sole custody

17. Howard and Marian separated after 17 years of marriage. Howard has to learn how to live as a single person again, since Marian is not there to take care of him. Howard has to learn to grocery shop, cook food, wash clothes, and iron. This couple is in which stage of separation?
    a. Early separation
    b. Mid-separation
    c. Late separation

18. Omar and Geneva divorced. The court ordered that Geneva would have sole custody of their two sons, Ahmad and Jalil. Omar was devastated. He picked the boys up from school one day and did not take them to Geneva's when he was supposed to. He moved them out of the state. This is a case of:
    a. Prickly child custody
    b. Child abduction
    c. Child support

19. George and Jane are the divorced parents of two children. Jane is the custodial parent, and George has been ordered to pay child support, but he does not. George believes that Jane turned the children against him, so he has distanced himself physically and emotionally from them. George represents the:
    a. Parent in pain
    b. Overloaded parent
    c. Vengeful parent

20. Esther and Woodrow are the divorced parents of two teenagers. They are completely unable to co-parent, and each tries to get the children to turn against the other parent. Esther and Woodrow are:
    a. Angry associates
    b. Fiery foes
    c. Dissolved duos

21. Reba and Shane are talking about the chances of a separated African-American couple reconciling. Reba believes that younger women are more likely to reconcile. Shane believes that older women are more likely to reconcile. Which of the following is true among blacks?
    a. Younger women are more likely than older women to reconcile
    b. Older women are more likely than younger women to reconcile
    c. Younger and older women are equally likely to reconcile

22. Cliff and Claire are the divorced parents of five children. At the time of the divorce, Cliff agreed to pay $1500 per month. That was before he started paying on his student loan. Now that he has to pay for the student loan, Cliff does not have enough money to meet his obligation to his family. Cliff represents the:
    a. Overloaded parent
    b. Irresponsible parent
    c. Vengeful parent

23. Michelle is a single parents and she is not receiving child support from her ex-husband. She wants to know if there are any laws that will help her. Michelle's neighbor tells her about the Child Support Enforcement Act which:
   a. Makes it a felony for anyone who crosses state lines to evade child support obligation
   b. Requires states to deduct payments from delinquent parents' pay checks
   c. Mandates periodic reviews of award levels

24. After 17 years of staying together for the 'children's sake,' Archie and Edith divorced. This illustrates the:
   a. Protect-the-kids divorce
   b. Late divorce
   c. Surprise divorce

25. Brad and Jennifer are talking about divorce and ethnicity. They want to know if some racial-ethnic groups are more likely to divorce. In fact, _____ are more likely to divorce.
   a. Blacks
   b. Whites
   c. Latinos

EXERCISES/APPLICATIONS

1. One explanation for rising divorce rates is changing cultural values. Americans are becoming more individualistic. Consider the messages sent by the media through television shows, movies, song lyrics, and magazines. What are common themes that may shape cultural values toward individualism and divorce?

2. In every country, women are initiating divorce for adultery, domestic violence, failure to provide financially, and abandonment. Are these good reasons to end a marriage? Why or why not?

CHAPTER 15 KEY TERMS CROSSWORD PUZZLE

Across
1. Ex is unable to let go
3. Stealing the kid
9. Divorce of irreconcilable differences
10. Payments to help with the kids
13. Hire someone to help exes reach agreement
14. Bonds with others

Down
2. Divorce station of detachment
4. Divorce station that is public
5. Determines who has the kids
6. Divorce station with separate lives
7. Spousal maintenance
8. Divorce station with financial debates
11. Partners live apart
12. Legal dissolution of marriage

POST-TEST

1. Sandra and Elvin are in the process of getting a divorce. They have been unable to agree on how the marital property should be divided so they hire a trained arbitrator to help them. This is called:
   a. Marital therapy
   b. Marital counseling
   c. Divorce mediation

2. Niles and Maris divorced 6 years ago. Now, their youngest daughter needs braces, and Maris believes that her ex-husband Niles should cover it. Niles believes that Maris should cover it out of the child support payments that he sends. They are in which stage of divorce?
   a. Community
   b. Psychic
   c. Economic

3. Son and Min Li are the divorced parents of three. The children divide their time between the parents, while Son and Min Li share in decisions about their upbringing. This reflects which custody arrangement?
   a. Split custody
   b. Joint custody
   c. Sole custody

4. Herman and Lillian are the divorced parents of two. Lillian has been receiving $125 per month in child support payments for the last 10 years. Which law will help Lillian get a raise in the child support payments to keep rate with inflation?
   a. 1984 Child Support Enforcement Amendment
   b. Family Support Act of 1988
   c. 1998 Deadbeat Parents Act

5. Will and Grace are the divorced parents of four children. Will has been ordered to pay child support, but he does not pay because he believes that welfare will take care of his children. Will represents the:
   a. Irresponsible parent
   b. Overloaded parent
   c. Vengeful parent

6. After years of living as a married heterosexual, one day Nathan revealed to his wife Sara that he was really gay and that he was tired of pretending. The two divorced but did not tell the children the real reason. This represents the:
   a. Disappearing parent divorce
   b. Surprise divorce
   c. Protect-the-kids divorce

7. Barney and Betty are the divorced parents of two. Both parents wanted sole custody. Betty was granted sole custody and Barney got visitation rights. Barney is hurt and feels that his visitation rights are unfair. He has distanced himself physically and emotionally from the children and does not pay child support. Barney represents the:
   a. Parent in pain
   b. Overloaded parent
   c. Vengeful parent

8. Ibrahim and Thiaba are divorced. They have a son and a daughter. By court order, the son lives with Ibrahim, and the daughter lives with Thiaba. This reflects which custody arrangement?
   a. Split custody
   b. Joint custody
   c. Sole custody

9. Timber has to give an in-class presentation of the relationship between divorce and education. Timber will report that:
   a. People with lower levels of education are more likely to divorce
   b. People with higher levels of education are more likely to divorce
   c. People with lower and higher levels of education are equally likely to divorce

10. When Daphne and Donnie were married, Daphne would often go on shopping sprees and spa days with her mother-in-law, Martina. When Daphne and Donnie divorced, all ties between Daphne and Martina were severed. This reflects the:
    a. Psychic divorce
    b. Community divorce
    c. Emotional divorce

11. Lionel and Jenny are a divorced couple. Both are remarried. Each year, Lionel, along with his new wife, and Jenny, along with her new husband, get together and take the kids on a fun, family cruise. Lionel and Jenny are:
    a. Perfect pals
    b. Cooperative colleagues
    c. Dissolved duos

12. Lorenzo and Lola are divorced. By the judge's orders, Lorenzo has full responsibility for raising the child, while Lola has some visitation rights. This reflects which custody arrangement?
    a. Split custody
    b. Joint custody
    c. Sole custody

13. Muhammad and Vashti are divorced. Muhammad still thinks of her as his wife, and he hopes to reconcile. Vashti just wants Muhammad to let go. Muhammad is experiencing:
    a. Separation anxiety
    b. Psychic divorce
    c. Divorce hangover

14. Once Thea left Denver and relocated to Los Angeles, she was able to establish a new life, separate from her ex-husband's. This reflects which station of divorce?
    a. Psychic
    b. Emotional
    c. Community

15. Since the divorce, Sam has not seen his wife or his children. They have broken off from one another entirely. As such they represent:
    a. Fiery foes
    b. Dissolved duos
    c. Angry associates

16. Oli and Mana are divorcing, and Mana has custody of the children. The judge orders Oli to pay Mana $1900 per month. This includes spousal maintenance and money to help with the children's expenses. This reflects:
    a. Alimony
    b. Child support
    c. Both a &b

17. Fred and Wilma are the divorced parents of one child. Wilma is the custodial parent, and Fred has been ordered to pay child support. Fred has remarried and is having difficulty supporting two households. He does not pay child support to Wilma. Fred represents the:
    a. Parent in pain
    b. Overloaded parent
    c. Vengeful parent

18. Shequetta and Tyrone are the divorced parents of 4 girls. The girls divide their time between their mother and father. Shequetta and Tyrone share in decisions about upbringing. This reflects which custody arrangement?
a. Split custody
b. Joint custody
c. Sole custody

19. Debra has stopped caring for her husband Raymond. She is detached from him. Which station of divorce does this represent?
a. Psychic
b. Emotional
c. Community

20. Desi and Lucy are both bitter about their divorce, which occurred 3 years ago. Whenever they speak with each other, they argue about past injuries that occurred during the marriage. They represent:
a. Angry associates
b. Fiery foes
c. Dissolved duos

21. Luke and Laura have separated after 19 years of marriage. During the marriage, they occupied very traditional gender roles. Now, Laura has to learn to live as a single again without Luke around. She has to learn how to mow the lawn, rake the leaves, and change her oil. This couple is in which stage of separation?
a. Early separation
b. Mid-separation
c. Late separation

22. Ridge no longer has intimate feelings for his wife Taylor. He believes that it was a mistake to marry her. Which station of divorce does this represent?
a. Psychic
b. Emotional
c. Community

23. Darren and Samantha Stevens went to court today and the judge determined that Darren must pay Samantha $735 a month in spousal maintenance. This refers to:
a. Alimony
b. Child support
c. Both a & b

24. George and Louise Jefferson went to court today to dissolve their marital union. Which station of divorce are the Jeffersons in?
    a. Legal
    b. Community
    c. Economic

25. Janet and Jack were married for twelve years when they decided to separate. Now, they are experiencing pressure from their parents, relatives, and friends to get back together. Both partners feel bad about the separation, and so they have a "pseudo-reconciliation" that does not last long. This occurs in which stage of separation:
    a. Early separation
    b. Mid-separation
    c. Late separation

SELF-ASSESSMENT:
WHAT ARE STRONG REASONS TO DIVORCE?

Directions: Read each statement. Put a check in the box to reflect whether or not the reason for divorce is strong or weak.

	Very Strong	Strong	Weak	Very Weak
My spouse physically assaulted me.				
My spouse had a sexual affair.				
I am unhappy.				
My spouse is selfish.				
My spouse is unemployed.				
My spouse has been convicted of a crime and sent to prison.				
My spouse has a drug problem.				
I am in love with someone else.				
My spouse and I are sexually incompatible.				
My spouse is controlling.				
My spouse had an emotional affair.				
My spouse raped me.				
My spouse has been accused of sexually molesting a child.				
My spouse has gained a tremendous amount of weight.				
My spouse likes to argue.				
My spouse has a drinking problem.				
My spouse does not respect me.				
My spouse has been disfigured in an accident.				
My spouse does not appreciate me.				
My spouse is no longer the person that I married.				
I do not trust my spouse.				
My spouse is unable to have children.				
My spouse has a gambling problem.				
My spouse lied to me.				
My spouse and I argue constantly.				
I am no longer attracted to my spouse.				

Key: Make a note of those statements that you feel are 'Very Strong' and 'Strong' reasons for divorce. Be sure to discuss these with your mate before you make the marriage vows, "For better or for worse."

ANSWERS

PRE-TEST

Answers	Page Numbers
1. C	460
2. A	459
3. C	469
4. B	454
5. C	472
6. B	458
7. A	459
8. B	455
9. B	458
10. C	459
11. C	460
12. B	459
13. A	459
14. B	459
15. C	467
16. C	469
17. C	459
18. B	470
19. A	472
20. B	460
21. B	455
22. A	472
23. B	472
24. B	474
25. A	463

KEY TERMS CROSSWORD PUZZLE

Across	Page Numbers
1. Divorce Hangover	467
3. Child Abduction	470
9. No Fault	459
10. Child Support	458
13. Mediation	481
14. Social Integration	461

Down	
2. Emotional	456
4. Community	459
5. Custody	468
6. Psychic	459
7. Alimony	468
8. Economic	459
11. Separation	454
12. Divorce	455

POST-TEST

Answers		Page Numbers
1.	C	481
2.	C	459
3.	B	469
4.	B	472
5.	A	472
6.	C	474
7.	A	472
8.	A	469
9.	A	464
10.	B	459
11.	A	460
12.	C	469
13.	C	455
14.	A	469
15.	B	460
16.	C	458
17.	B	472
18.	B	469
19.	B	456
20.	A	460
21.	C	454
22.	B	456
23.	A	458
24.	A	459
25.	B	454

16

REMARRIAGE AND STEPFAMILIES

CHAPTER OBJECTIVES

Upon reading Chapter Sixteen, students should be able to:

1. Discuss the prevalence and characteristics of stepfamilies.

2. Discuss the prevalence and characteristics of remarriages.

3. Explain remarriage as a process.

4. Compare and contrast first marriages and remarriages.

5. Discuss the most common myths associated with remarriage.

6. Compare and contrast the different types of step-families.

7. Discuss parenting roles in gay and lesbian step-families.

8. Compare and contrast step-families and nuclear families.

9. Explain the stepfamily cycle.

10. Describe life in stepfamilies.

11. Explain how living in stepfamilies impacts children.

12. Identify characteristics of successful stepfamilies.

CHAPTER OVERVIEW

A **stepfamily** is a household in which two adults are biological or adaptive parents with a child from a previous relationship, who elect to marry or cohabit. The U.S. has the highest remarriage rate in the world. Nearly 85% of people who divorce marry again. Typically, both men and women remarry within three years. The presence of children lowers the likelihood of remarriage. Divorced people tend to marry other divorced people. Remarriage may involve six stages: *emotional remarriage* (divorced person reestablishes a bond of attraction, commitment and trust with a new partner), *psychic remarriage* (identity changes from a single individual to part of a couple), *community remarriage* (friendship circles change), *parental remarriage* (relationship between partner and the new spouse's children develop), *economic remarriage* (household is reestablished as an economically productive unit), and *legal remarriage* (legal rights and responsibilities of the family members are defined). Compared to first marriages, family composition is more diverse; role expectations are less defined; family members may be at different points of the life cycle; and there are more stress factors and resources in remarriages. **Half-siblings** are brothers and sisters who share one biological parent. There are four common myths that promote dangerous stepfamily expectations: *the nuclear family myth* (family members feel close to one another, children show deference to parents and nonresidential parents disappear), the *compensation myth* (the new mate is everything that the problematic old mate wasn't), *the instant love myth* (new stepparents presume an intimacy and authority they have not yet earned), and *the rescue fantasy* (stepparents will rescue children from the negative, lenient, or ineffectual discipline of custodial parents). Remarried couples reportedly share decision-making more equally than in first marriages. Remarried husbands do more housework than their first-time married counterparts. The average duration of 1st and 2nd marriages that end in divorce is about 8 years. Women who have *intermarital* birth (giving birth between marriages) are more likely to divorce.

When a stepfamily is formed, new family networks emerge, which are often traced in a **genogram**, a diagram showing the biological relationships between family members. There are three basic types of step-families: **mother-stepfather family** (all children are biological children of the mother and the stepchildren of the father), **father-stepmother family** (all children are biological children of the father and stepchildren of the mother) and **joint stepfamily** (at least one child is the biological child of both parents, at least one child is the biological child of only one parent and the stepchild of the other parent, and no other type of child is present). In a *complex stepfamily*, both adults have children from previous marriages. In *joint-step-adoptive* families and *joint biological-step-adoptive families*, at least one child is a biological child of one parent and a stepchild of the other parent, and one or both parents have adopted at least one child. Gay and lesbian stepfamilies encounter triple stigmatization. They are stigmatized for their homosexuality, seen as deficient compared with nuclear families, and criticized for parenthood. There are three distinct stepparent roles in lesbian families: *co-parent family* (the non-biological mother is a supporter, helper, and consultant to the biological mother), *stepmother family* (the non-biological mother does most of the traditional mothering tasks, but the biological mother retains decision making power), and *co-mother family* (both mothers have equal rights and responsibilities in everyday decisions and childrearing).

Stepfamilies differ from non-divorced families in that: stepfamilies have a complex structure; a stepfamily must cope with unique tasks; stepfamilies often experience more stress than nuclear families; satisfactory stepfamily integration generally takes years to achieve; relationships may end abruptly as others spring up; there may be continuous transitions and adjustments instead of stability; there is less cohesiveness in stepfamilies; stepfamilies require more flexibility; there are often unrealistic expectations; there is no shared family history; there are many loyalty conflicts; and the roles in the stepfamily are often ambiguous. The process of becoming a stepfamily involves three stages. The *early stage* is characterized by fantasies, confusion, and slowly getting to know other family members. The *middle stage* involves restructuring the family. In the *late stage*, the family achieves its own identity. There are a number of problems in merging two households after a remarriage. These include: naming, sexual boundaries, legal issues, distributing economic and emotional resources, establishing discipline and closeness, developing parent-child relationships, children's adjustment, and intergenerational relationships.

Although the results are mixed, many studies show that children in remarried families don't do as well as children in nuclear families. They tend to have more problems academically and show more problem behaviors. The *cumulative effects hypothesis* suggests that children who undergo multiple transitions experience more emotional and behavioral difficulties because the problems snowball. *Risk and resilience theories* suggest that the effects of remarriage on children reflect both costs and benefits. Children are more resilient when there are fewer costs and more benefits. *Social capital models* maintain that children in stepfamily households have more problems than children in non-divorce households if parenting is inadequate, if the parents are not involved in the children's academic life, and if there's tension between the adults.

The seven characteristics of successful step-families are: realistic expectations, a chance for children to mourn their losses, a strong couple relationship, slow proceeding of the step-parenting role, gradual transition of the stepparent into the disciplinarian role, the development of their own rituals, and satisfactory arrangements between the children's households.

PRE-TEST

1. Lois and Clark are establishing commitment and trust in their relationship. Which stage of remarriage does this represent?
   a. Psychic
   b. Emotional
   c. Community

2. Phoebe and Rachel are a lesbian couple. They live together with Phoebe's daughter from a previous relationship. They represent a/an:
   a. Extended family
   b. Stepfamily
   c. Nuclear family

3. Enrique and Anna Olvino are a married couple. In the Olvino family, all of the children are the biological children of Anna and the stepchildren of Enrique. This type of step-family is a:
   a. Joint step family
   b. Father-stepmother family
   c. Mother-stepfather family

4. Yin and Tang were just married. Yin is adjusting to her new role as wife and is beginning to identify herself as a part of a couple. Which stage of remarriage is represented here?
   a. Psychic
   b. Community
   c. Emotional

5. Alice and Mel are having a debate about remarriage rates around the world. Mel thinks that the rates are highest in the U.K. Alice thinks they are highest in the U.S. Which is true?
   a. The U.S. remarriage rate is the highest in the world
   b. The U.K. remarriage rate is the highest in the world
   c. The U.S. and the U.K. remarriage rates are equal

6. Ruth believes that mothers of young children should not remarry. She thinks that it will have a negative effect on the child. Ruth's daughter Amy explains that remarriage can have a positive effect on children if there are more benefits than costs. Amy's idea is supported by which theory?
   a. Social capital models
   b. Risk and resilience theories
   c. Cumulative effect hypothesis

7. Eileen and Barbara are a lesbian couple who live together with Eileen's 3 children. Both mothers have equal rights and responsibilities in raising the children. This represents which type of family?
    a. Stepmother family
    b. Co-mother family
    c. Co-parent family

8. Alberto and Beatriz are a newly married couple. They have moved to a new neighborhood and joined a new church. In so doing, the couple has made new friends. They do not see their old friends as much as they used to. This couple is in which stage of remarriage?
    a. Community
    b. Psychic
    c. Emotional

9. Brian and Claude are brothers. They have the same father but different mothers. Brian and Claude are:
    a. Half-siblings
    b. Step-siblings
    c. Both a & b

10. Pauline and Marvin are a married couple. When they married, Pauline had one daughter named Michelle from a previous marriage. Last year, Pauline and Marvin had a child together and named her Cherie. Now, Pauline, Marvin, Michelle, and Cherie all live together. Which type of step family is represented?
    a. Mother-stepfather family
    b. Father-stepmother family
    c. Joint stepfamily

11. Lola and Sonny are a remarrying couple, and they both have children from previous marriages. The family, made up of Lola, Sonny, and their children, has established a unique identity. This family is in which stage of the stepfamily cycle?
    a. Early
    b. Middle
    c. Later

12. Monique and Rich were recently married, and now Monique has a step-daughter. Monique picks her step-daughter up from cheerleading practice every Tuesday and Thursday evening. Monique says that this gives them time to bond. This represents which stage of remarriage?
    a. Parental
    b. Community
    c. Legal

13. Carla is divorced. She wants to remarry soon. She believes that her second husband will be everything that her ex-husband was not. Which myth does this represent?
    a. Instant love myth
    b. Rescue fantasy
    c. Compensation myth

14. Since Heather and Derrick married, Heather's ex-husband has stopped paying child-support for his children. This has put a tremendous stress on Heather and Derrick's marital resources. This represents which stage of remarriage?
    a. Economic
    b. Legal
    c. Community

15. Ronesha and Jaime are a remarrying couple. They both believe that they will love each other's children and be loved by them. Which stage in the stepfamily cycle are they in?
    a. Early
    b. Middle
    c. Later

16. Tammy and Toya are a lesbian couple. Toya has three children from a previous relationship. While Tammy takes care of the cooking and cleaning, Toya maintains decision making power over the children. This type of family is:
    a. Co-mother family
    b. Stepmother family
    c. Co-parent family

17. Angela is engaged to marry Tony. She believes that once she marries Tony she will have a positive impact on his children because she will give them the discipline that they need. This represents which myth?
    a. Instant love myth
    b. Rescue fantasy
    c. Nuclear family myth

18. Emmanuel and Luella Robinson are a married couple. In the Robinson family, all of the children are the biological children of Emmanuel and the stepchildren of Luella. This illustrates which stepfamily?
    a. Father-stepmother family
    b. Joint stepfamily
    c. Mother-stepfather family

19. Marquita lives in a step-family. Tawanna lives with her biological parents. Which girl is most at risk for sexual abuse?
    a. Marquita
    b. Tawanna
    c. They face an equal risk

20. Seiku is Asian-American. Sky is an American Indian teen. Which teen is most likely to live in a step-family?
    a. Seiku
    b. Sky
    c. They are equally likely

21. Ed is presenting a paper in class tomorrow on the duration of marriages and remarriages. Ed will report that:
    a. First marriages that end in divorce tend to last longer then second marriages that end in divorce
    b. Second marriages that end in divorce tend to last longer than first marriages that end in divorce.
    c. First and second marriages that end in divorce last about the same length of time

22. Stacy wants to give her grandmother a very special gift for her 96th birthday. Stacy makes a diagram which shows the biological relationships among family members. Stacy made a:
    a. Genogram
    b. Family tree
    c. Family-gram

23. Elsa is a teen-aged girl, and her mother just remarried. Lionel is a teen-aged boy, and his mother just remarried. Which child is most likely to have a negative reaction to the remarriage?
    a. Elsa
    b. Lionel
    c. They are equally likely

24. Ian just married Jude. After the honeymoon, Ian tells Jude that she is the co-benefactor of his estate. In the event of his death, she and his ex-wife will split everything 50/50. This represents which stage of remarriage?
    a. Economic
    b. Legal
    c. Community

25. Wanda recently married Lawrence and moved in with him and his children. Wanda is upset by how often Lawrence's ex-wife calls or comes by the house for the kids. Wanda had thought that the ex-wife would leave them alone. Wanda was disillusioned by which myth?
    a. Nuclear family myth
    b. Compensation myth
    c. Instant love myth

EXERCISES/APPLICATIONS

1. In remarriages, there is an absence of socially prescribed guidelines for relationships within remarriages. What does the ideal step-family look like? Consider the role expectations and boundaries that you would have for a step-family. Include expectations for mother, father, step-mother, step-father, ex-husband, ex-wife, half-siblings, step-siblings, step aunts and uncles and step grandparents.

2. The U.S. has the highest remarriage rate in the world? Is this reflected through the media? How many family television shows and movies portray step-families? What myths and stereotypes are portrayed on such shows?

CHAPTER 16 KEY TERMS CROSSWORD PUZZLE

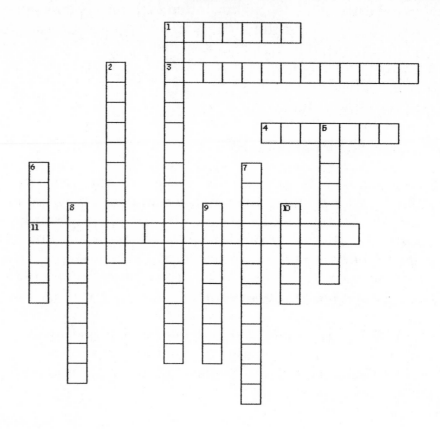

Across

1. Say 'I do' again
3. Models explaining how divorce impacts children
4. Stepfamily with biological kids on both sides
11. Hypothesis explaining snowball effect on children of divorce

Down

1. Theories exploring the costs and benefits of divorce
2. Household with a couple & kids from before
5. Stage of remarriage in which relationship is built with stepchild
6. Stage of remarriage involving identity change
7. Children who share one biological parent
8. Stage of remarriage involving trust
9. Diagram showing family relationships
10. Stage of remarriage outlining new responsibilities

POST-TEST

1. Raquel lives in a step-family. Joyce lives with her biological parents. Which girl is most at risk for sexual abuse?
   a. Raquel
   b. Joyce
   c. They face an equal risk

2. Henry recently visited his son's school to add his new wife on the list as a guardian. As a guardian, Henry's new wife has the right to pick her step-son up from school early, sign permission slips, and meet with teachers. This represents which stage of remarriage?
   a. Legal
   b. Economic
   c. Community

3. Rita was married before, and her ex-husband was loud, rude, and irresponsible. She believes that her new husband is going to be everything that her old husband was not. Which myth does this represent?
   a. Instant love myth
   b. Rescue Fantasy
   c. Compensation myth

4. Emma and Clara are sisters who have the same mother, but different fathers. Emma and Clara are:
   a. Half-siblings
   b. Step-siblings
   c. Both a & b

5. Tabitha and Karen are a lesbian couple. Karen has a son from a previous relationship. Both Karen and Tabitha have equal rights and responsibilities in child-rearing and decision making. This represents the:
   a. Co-parent family
   b. Co-mother family
   c. Stepmother family

6. Doug and Lisa Diekow are a married couple. In the Diekow family, all of the children are the biological children of Lisa and the stepchildren of Doug. This type of step-family is
   a. Joint step family
   b. Father-stepmother family
   c. Mother-stepfather family

7. Wendy is a teen-aged girl, and her mother just remarried. Cal is a teen-aged boy, and his mother just remarried. Which child is most likely to have a negative reaction to the remarriage?
   a. Wendy
   b. Cal
   c. They are equally likely

8. Tiffany is a single mother. She believes that because the benefits outweigh the costs, remarriage would be beneficial to her children. Tiffany's ideas coincide with which theory?
   a. Social capital models
   b. Risk and resilience theories
   c. Cumulative effect hypothesis

9. Farzan is about to marry Azza and become a husband and step-father. Farzan believes that he is just what Azza's children need to grow up to be obedient and disciplined. This represents which myth?
   a. Rescue fantasy
   b. Compensation myth
   c. Instant love myth

10. Bill and Hillary are a remarrying couple and they both have children from previous marriages. The family made up of Bill, Hillary, and their children has established a unique identity. This family is in which stage of the stepfamily cycle?
    a. Early
    b. Middle
    c. Later

11. Debra and Gwen are a lesbian couple. Debra has children from a previous relationship. While Gwen takes care of cooking, cleaning, and helping the children with homework, Debra retains decision making power. This reflects which form of family?
    a. Step-mother family
    b. Co-mother family
    c. Co-Parent family

12. Howard and Marian are a married couple. Each month, Howard has to pay $1500 in child support to his ex-wife. This puts financial stress on Howard and Marian's marriage. This stage of remarriage is called:
    a. Parental
    b. Economic
    c. Legal

13. Mike and Robin Tyson are a married couple. In the Tyson family, all of the children are the biological children of Mike and the stepchildren of Robin. This illustrates which stepfamily?
    a. Father-stepmother family
    b. Joint stepfamily
    c. Mother-stepfather family

14. Cyndi married Bob and moved in with him and his children. Cyndi cannot believe how disrespectful Bob's children are to him and to her. Cyndi expected that the children would be more polite. Cyndi was disillusioned by which myth?
    a. Compensation myth
    b. Nuclear family myth
    c. Instant love myth

15. Thomasina is interested in serial monogamists and remarriages. Tomorrow, she will be presenting a paper in class on the duration of 2nd and 3rd marriages. Thomasina will report that:
    a. Second marriages that end in divorce tend to last longer then third marriages that end in divorce
    b. Third marriages that end in divorce tend to last longer than second marriages that end in divorce.
    c. Second and third marriages that end in divorce last about the same length of time

16. Phillip and Edina were recently married and now Phillip has a step-son. Phillip tries to attend all of his stepson's little league games because it gives him a chance to develop a relationship with the boy. This represents which stage of remarriage?
    a. Community
    b. Legal
    c. Parental

17. Martin and Gina are a married couple. When they first married, Gina had one son already named Tommy. Since then, Gina and Martin have had a little girl named Pam. Now Martin, Gina, Tommy, and Pam all live together. This represents which type of stepfamily?
    a. Joint
    b. Mother-stepfather family
    c. Father-stepmother family

18. Chandler and Ross are a gay couple. They live together with Ross's son from a previous relationship. They represent a/an:
    a. Nuclear family
    b. Stepfamily
    c. Extended family

19. Reggie and Tia are a remarrying couple. They both believe that they will love each other's children and be loved by them. Which stage in the stepfamily cycle are they in?
    a. Early
    b. Middle
    c. Later

20. Lauren and Paul are a newly married couple. Since they married, Lauren no longer hangs out with the married couples that she had befriended with her ex-husband. Lauren and Paul have developed a new network of friends. This represents which stage of remarriage?
    a. Psychic
    b. Community
    c. Emotional

21. Over the holidays, Shay wants to develop a project to involve the entire family. She decides that the family will create a diagram that shows the biological relationships among family members. Shay wants to create a:
    a. Genogram
    b. Family-gram
    c. Family tree

22. Ali and Naama were recently married. Naama is gradually beginning to adjust to her role as wife. Since she realizes that she is a part of a couple and not a single person, she checks with her husband before she makes plans. This represents which stage of remarriage?
    a. Psychic
    b. Community
    c. Emotional

23. Tanisha is a divorced woman who wants children. Lanita is a divorced woman who does not want children. Who is more likely to remarry?
    a. Tanisha
    b. Lanita
    c. They are equally likely

24. Dean and Swan are a married couple. This is their first marriage. Larry and Kim are a married couple and this is their second marriage. Which couple is more likely to share in decision making?
    a. Dean and Swan
    b. Larry and Kim
    c. They are equally likely

25. Nyree and Todd love to look at each other. Their physical attraction is extremely strong. Which stage of remarriage does this represent?
   a. Community
   b. Psychic
   c. Emotional

SELF-ASSESSMENT:
HOW STEPPED IS YOUR FAMILY?

Directions: Read each statement. Put a check in the box to reflect whether or not the statement is true or false.

	True	False
I have a step-mother.		
I have a step-father.		
I have a step-brother.		
I have a step-sister.		
I have a step-aunt.		
I have a step-uncle.		
I have a step-cousin.		
I have a step-grandmother.		
I have a step-grandfather.		
I have a step-niece.		
I have a step-nephew.		
I have more than one step-mother.		
I have more than one step-father.		
I have more than one step-brother.		
I have more than one step-sister.		
I have more than one step aunt.		
I have more than one step-uncle.		
I have more than one step-cousin.		
I have more than one step-grandmother.		
I have more than one step-grandfather.		
I have more than one step-niece.		
I have more than one step-nephew.		

Key: Give yourself 1 point for every statement that you checked as 'True.' A score of 22 represents an extremely stepped family. A score of 0 represents a stepless family.

ANSWERS

PRE-TEST

Answers	Page Numbers
1. B	490
2. B	487
3. C	496
4. A	490
5. A	487
6. B	508
7. B	497
8. A	490
9. A	492
10. A	496
11. C	499
12. A	491
13. C	494
14. A	491
15. A	499
16. B	497
17. B	494
18. A	496
19. A	503
20. B	497
21. C	495
22. A	496
23. A	507
24. B	491
25. A	494

KEY TERMS CROSSWORD PUZZLE

Across	Page Numbers
1. Remarry	490
3. Social capital	508
4. Complex	496
11. Cumulative effects	508

Down	
1. Risk and resilience	508
2. Stepfamily	487
5. Parental	491
6. Psychic	491
7. Half-siblings	492
8. Emotional	490
9. Genogram	496
10. Legal	491

POST-TEST

Answers	Page Numbers
1. A	503
2. A	491
3. C	494
4. A	492
5. B	497
6. C	496
7. A	507
8. B	508
9. A	494
10. C	499
11. A	497
12. B	491
13. A	496
14. A	494
15. A	495
16. C	491
17. A	496
18. B	487
19. A	499
20. B	490
21. A	496
22. A	490
23. A	488
24. B	494
25. C	490

17

FAMILIES IN LATER LIFE

CHAPTER OBJECTIVES

Upon reading Chapter Seventeen, students should be able to:

1. Discuss the demographics of the aging population in the U.S.

2. Discuss the physical and mental health of the aging population.

3. Discuss the social status of the elderly.

4. Discuss ageism and stereotypes among the elderly.

5. Describe work and retirement patterns among the elderly.

6. Discuss grandparenting among the elderly.

7. Compare and contrast family relationships among the elderly.

8. Discuss dying, death, and bereavement among the elderly.

9. Discuss widowhood among the elderly.

10.   Compare and contrast family caregiving patterns.

CHAPTER OVERVIEW

The number of people reaching the age of 65 is increasing. The average **life expectancy** (the average length of time people of the same age will live) for people born in 1990 in America is 78 years. The number of *elderly people*, those aged 65 and over, has increased, while the proportion of younger people has decreased. **Gerontologists** (scientists who study aging) suggest that because of differences in independent living, employment, and health care needs, the elderly should be divided into 3 categories: the *young old* (aged 65-74), the *old-old* (aged 75-84) and the *oldest old* (aged 85 and older). Living longer has created millions of **later-life families** (families that are beyond the childrearing years). In the U. S., and in most countries, women live longer than men. Physical decline is normal and inevitable across age groups. Two of the most common mental health problems for older people are **depression** (mental disorder characterized by pervasive sadness) and **dementia** (loss of mental abilities that most commonly occur late in life). The most common form of dementia is **Alzheimer's disease** (progressive, degenerative disorder that attacks the brain and impairs memory, thinking, and behavior). The status of the elderly has declined since the turn of the 20th century. The U.S. is a youth-oriented society and negative attitudes toward aging prevail. *Ageism* refers to discrimination against people on the basis of age. Although the data shows otherwise, many people continue to believe that older Americans are less intelligent, less competent, and less active than young people. Stereotypes and negative images of the elderly are created and perpetuated in the media.

Retirement, the exit from the paid labor force, is a recent phenomenon. Many people are working beyond the age of 65 because **social security** (a public retirement pension system administered by the federal government) only replaces a fraction of pre-retirement income; the Social Security Administration eliminated penalties for later retirement; older people need the health benefits that come with paid labor; there is an increased demand for labor; many companies have eliminated pension plans; and many elderly people can not afford to retire. Retirement presents more financial problems to women than men.

The most common styles of grandparenting are *remote* (grandparents and grandchildren see each other infrequently), *companionate and supportive* (grandparents see their grandchildren often but do not seek authority), *involved and influential* (grandparents play an active role in raising their grandchildren), *advisory and authoritative* (grandparent is an adviser), and *cultural transmitters* (grandparents transmit cultural values and norms). An emerging grandparenting role is that of *surrogate*, in which the grandparent provides regular care or replaces the parents in raising the child. There are three categories of surrogates: *custodial grandparents* (have a legal relationship with their grandchildren through adoption, guardianship, or custody), *living-with grandparents* (have the children in their own home or live in a home maintained by the grandchild's parents) and *day-care grandparents* (assume responsibility for the grandchildren until the parents come home from work).

The U-shaped pattern of marital satisfaction suggests that marital satisfaction is high in the early years, drops during childrearing, and rises after children leave home. Adult children who live nearby tend to have closer relationships to parents than adult children who live far away. Parents tend to help the children with the most need. Parent-child relationships often involve **intergenerational ambivalence** (contradictions that arise from structured kinship roles and personal emotions). Sibling relationships in later life fall into five groups: *intimate*

253

siblings (best friends), *congenial siblings* (good friends), *loyal* (available only because of family bonds), *apathetic* (rarely think about one another and have little contact), and *hostile* (resentful and negative).

Physicians and other health-care professionals often use the term *dying trajectory* to describe the manner in which a very ill person is expected to die. In a *lingering trajectory*, medical personnel do all that they can to treat the patient, but ultimately custodial care predominates. The *quick trajectory* is an acute crisis in which staff works feverishly to preserve the patient's life and well-being. There are five stages of dying: denial, anger, bargaining, depression, and acceptance. Some argue that this model is not entirely applicable to the elderly. Although many elderly parents and relatives die in hospitals and nursing homes, **hospice** (a place for care of dying patients that stresses pain control, security, and companionship) provides an alternative by making the patient more comfortable. Dealing with death involves **bereavement**, the state of having been deprived of a loved one. Two common expressions of bereavement are **grief** (emotional response to loss) and **mourning** (customary outward expression of grief). There are clusters or phases of grief. People respond *initially* with shock, numbness, and disbelief, followed by a feeling of sorrow. In the *intermediate* stage of grief, people often idealize a loved one. In the *final stage* of grief, recovery and reorganization occurs. *Thanatologists*, social scientists who study death and grief, encourage parents to talk about death with children openly and honestly. There are more widows than widowers. Some widows and many widowers begin to date again after losing a mate. Companionship is the most common reason for dating.

The *sandwich generation* refers to mid-life men and women who feel caught between meeting responsibilities to both their own children and to their aging parents. Many are becoming "club sandwich families" as children, parents, grand-parents, and great-grandparents all live together. A **caregiver** is a person, paid or unpaid, who attends to the needs of someone who is old, sick, or disabled. Most typically, the caregivers of the elderly are the female oldest child. There are five types of caregiving for elderly parents: *routine* (incorporates regular assistance to the parent in his or her ongoing activities), *backup* (steps in when needed), *circumscribed* (limited assistance but predictable and agreed upon), *sporadic* (provides services at own convenience), and *disassociation* (cannot be counted on at all). Families are the primary source of assistance for the frail elderly.

PRE-TEST

1. Alberta lives in Florida, and her grandchildren live with their parents in Wyoming. They see each other once every 2 years during the holidays. Their relationships is:
   a) Involved and influential
   b) Remote
   c) Companionate and Supportive

2. Nina found out that her brother died, and she cried. This illustrates:
   a) Grief
   b) Mourning
   c) Ambiguity

3. Now that Clinton is retired, he qualifies for the government's public retirement pension system which is called:
   a) Medicaid
   b) Medicare
   c) Social Security

4. Geraldo is 74 and Ouida is 68. They are a married couple well beyond the childrearing years. Their children are 48, 43, and 37 years old. They constitute a:
   a) Nuclear family
   b) Later-life family
   c) Boomerang family

5. Lanita and Walter are grandparents that live down the street from their children and grandchildren. Lanita and Walter see their grandchildren often, but don't seek authority. This grandparenting style is:
   a) Involved and influential
   b) Remote
   c) Companionate and supportive

6. Hubert and Genie have two children: Margaret and Reginald. Because Margaret is the female, Hubert and Genie expect her to care for them. Although Margaret loves her parents, she resents this demand. This contradiction reflects:
   a) Intergenerational ambivalence
   b) Multi-generational support
   c) Boomerang generation

7. Twee has been declared mentally incompetent, and the courts have granted guardianship of Twee's children to Twee's mother. Twee's mother is a _____ grandparent.
   a) Custodial
   b) Living-with
   c) Day-care

8. Martin was 84 years old when he had a heart attack. Medical personnel worked hard to keep Martin alive, but he died while they were working. This represents which dying trajectory?
   a) Lingering trajectory
   b) Quick trajectory
   c) Both a & b

9. Hector is presenting a paper on widowhood in class tomorrow. Hector will report that:
   a) There are more widows than widowers
   b) There are more widowers than widows
   c) There are an equal number of widows and widowers

10. Tonya just found out that she was dying. Her first reaction was:
    a) Anger
    b) Bargaining
    c) Denial

11. Oliver and Wanda have been married for 55 years. Their levels of marital satisfaction started off high, dropped, and are now high again. This pattern is called:
    a) Empty nest syndrome
    b) U-shaped curve
    c) S-shaped curve

12. Laverne and Shirley are sisters in their late nineties. They both view one another as best friends and close confidants. These women are:
    a) Intimate siblings
    b) Congenial siblings
    c) Loyal siblings

13. After the interview, the human resources director told her assistant that it would be unwise to hire Angelo because he is "too old." This reflects:
    a) Ageism
    b) Ageophobia
    c) Age Harassment

14. Kenneth is 67 years old and is experiencing a sudden loss of mental abilities. This loss may be:
a) Dementia
b) Grief
c) Depression

15. Ivanla has incorporated caring for her aging mother as a part of her everyday life. Ivanla visits her mom everyday and does whatever needs to be done. This represents which caregiving style?
a) Backup
b) Routine help
c) Circumscribed

16. It has been twenty-five years since Tina spoke with her sister Rose. The last time they talked, Rose accused Tina of sleeping with her husband. Neither of the sisters have forgiven or forgotten. They are:
a) Apathetic siblings
b) Loyal siblings
c) Hostile siblings

17. Mary Kay and Ashley were born in 1990. The average length of time people born in that year will live to be is 78. This refers to their:
a) Life expectancy
b) Death expectancy
c) Mortality rate

18. Grady is 91 years old. Lately, he has been experience a pervasive sense of sadness that prevents him from sleeping and enjoying his favorite pastime. Grady is experiencing:
a) Dementia
b) Depression
c) Alzheimer's

19. Quinita takes care of her grandchildren everyday while her daughter and son-in-law work. Quinita is which type of grandparent?
a) Day-care
b) Living-with
c) Custodial

20. When Nabeel announced that he was exiting the paid labor force, his company gave him a party and presented him with a watch. This marked Nabeel's:
a) Retirement
b) Social security
c) Pension

21. Sylvester does not like his brother at all. Yet, Sylvester visits his brother once a week in the nursing home and pays for his brother's care. Sylvester and his brother both believe that this is what family members should do for one another. They represent:
    a) Intimate siblings
    b) Apathetic siblings
    c) Loyal siblings

22. Aylen is a Native American grandfather of 12. He often provides the grandchildren with information about their history and cultural practices through storytelling. This represents which style of grandparenting?
    a) Cultural transmitters
    b) Remote
    c) Companionate and Supportive

23. Michaela's daughter died, and she has taken in her grandchildren. In replacing her daughter as a caretaker, Michaela is a:
    a) Cultural transmitter
    b) Surrogate
    c) Caregiver

24. Carlita and Ola are headed to a conference for people who study the biological, psychological, and social aspects of aging. The conference is for:
    a) Thanotologists
    b) Gerontologists
    c) Ageologists

25. Esther is 96 years old. She is a part of which age group:
    a) Young-old
    b) Old-old
    c) Oldest-old

EXERCISES/APPLICATIONS

1.   What personal experiences have you had with others in which it was suggested that young is preferable to looking old? How have such experiences impacted your outlook on aging?

2.   There are many negative stereotypes associated with aging. Consider some of your favorite television shows, movies, and commercials. How are the elderly portrayed? Is there a difference between how older men are portrayed and how older women are portrayed? Have you seen any positive portrayals of the elderly lately?

CHAPTER 17 KEY TERMS CROSSWORD PUZZLE

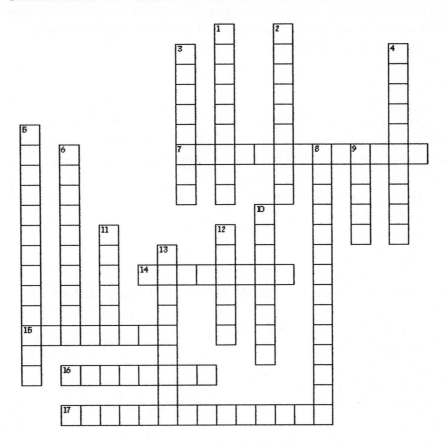

Across

7. Studies death
14. Outward expression of grief
15. Best friend siblings
16. Generation between parents and kids
17. Public retirement pension

Down

1. Grandparent providing regular care
2. Indifferent siblings
3. Loss of mental abilities
4. Pervasive sadness
5. Studies aging
6. Exit from the paid labor force
8. Average time to live
9. Emotional response to loss
10. A 65 year old
11. Discrimination against the elderly
12. First stage of dying
13. Good friend siblings

POST-TEST

1. Lauren takes care of her granddaughter every day when her son and daughter-in-law are at work. Lauren enjoys the company, and she also likes to help the young couple economically. Lauren is which type of grandparent?
   a. Living-with
   b. Day care
   c. Custodial

2. Sol is a 66 year old mid-level manager. Lately, Sol has been experiencing a pervasive sadness that prevents him from sleeping, eating, and completing his tasks at work. Sol is experiencing:
   a. Depression
   b. Dementia
   c. Alzheimer's disease

3. Betty is an 80 year old grandmother. Betty is a part of which age group.
   a. Young-old
   b. Old-old
   c. Oldest-old

4. Recently, Greg and Marsha were arrested for selling drugs. Since they were incarcerated, Marsha's mother has been taking care of the children. Marsha's mother is a:
   a. Cultural transmitter
   b. Surrogate
   c. Guardian

5. Mr. and Mrs. Huang have been married for 46 years. Because of their busy careers, they never had children. Now, they are both planning to retire so that they can travel the world together. They represent a/n:
   a. Extended family
   b. Nuclear family
   c. Later life family

6. Tim left the paid labor force in 2004. Three years later, his wife Ericka did the same. This suggests that both Tim and Ericka have experienced:
   a. Retirement
   b. Pensions
   c. Caregiving

7. Inez's daughter had a near-fatal accident. Since then, a judge granted Inez legal guardianship of her grandchildren. Inez is a _____ grandparent.
    a. Custodial
    b. Living-with
    c. Day-care

8. Megan's husband died yesterday, and she will wear black for one year. This illustrates:
    a. Mourning
    b. Grief
    c. Ambiguity

9. Skylar is the keynote speaker for the organization of social scientists who study aging. The organization is for:
    a. Thanotologists
    b. Gerontologists
    c. Ageologists

10. Winter and Summer are sisters who believe that blood is thicker than water. That means that even though the sisters do not like one another, they help one another out as much as they can because they are family. These siblings are:
    a. Apathetic
    b. Congenial
    c. Loyal

11. Zeke takes his mother out every once in a while and always at his own convenience. The family cannot count on Zeke to schedule any caregiving. Zeke's caregiving style is:
    a. Routine
    b. Sporadic
    c. Circumscribed

12. Cheyenne and Jake are debating which racial-ethnic group is most likely to have positive sibling relationships. Cheyenne says whites, Jake says blacks. Which is it?
    a. Whites
    b. Blacks
    c. Whites and Blacks are equally likely

13. Salaam died nine months after his cancer diagnosis. He went through all of the stages of dying. As such, the last stage that Salaam went through was:
    a. Acceptance
    b. Depression
    c. Bargaining

14. Blanche believes that the company did not hire her because she is a senior citizen. Blanche suspects:
    a. Ageism
    b. Ageophobia
    c. Age Harassment

15. Amina just found out that she is going to be a grandmother. When asked which grandparenting style she will adopt, Amina says that she will adopt the one that is most common. Amina's grandparenting style will be:
    a. Involved and influential
    b. Companionate and supportive
    c. Advisory and authoritative

16. Annica is 68 years old and retired. Each month, Annica receives a $700 check from the government's public retirement pension system known as:
    a. Medicare
    b. Medicaid
    c. Social security

17. The average woman will live to be older than the average man. This suggests that women have a higher:
    a. Life expectancy
    b. Death expectancy
    c. Mortality rate

18. Big Mama is an African American grandmother. When she gets to see her grandchildren, she often tells them stories about how her great-great grandparents escaped from slavery, learned to read, and opened a school. Big Mama's grandparenting style is:
    a. Involved and influential
    b. Cultural transmitter
    c. Companionate and Supportive

19. Akashi recognizes that as the oldest male, he is expected to provide for his parents in their old age. However, Akashi resents this demand. This contradiction represents:
    a. Mutigenerational ties
    b. Intergenerational ambivalence
    c. Boomerang generation

20. Tyrone and Loretta have been married for 30 years. Their levels of marital satisfaction started off high, dropped, and are now high again. This pattern is called:
    a. U-shaped curve
    b. Empty nest syndrome
    c. S-shaped curve

21. Lisette cannot believe that her 82 year old grandmother is dating! When she asks her grandmother why she dates, her grandmother tells her that she dates for the same reason that most elderly people date. That reason is:
    a. Sex
    b. Companionship
    c. Financial gain

22. Vanessa died with cancer. Medical personnel did all that they could to treat her, and then she lived with her children for 14 months before dying. This represents which dying trajectory?
    a. Lingering trajectory
    b. Quick trajectory
    c. Both a & b

23. Peter is seven years old, and he is fascinated with death and dying. He tells his parents that when he grows up, he wants to conduct scientific research on death. Peter wants to be a:
    a. Thanotologist
    b. Gerontologist
    c. Caregiver

24. Doug and his brother Michael rarely think about each other. They have had very little contact with each other since their mother died 26 years ago. These brothers are:
    a. Congenial
    b. Hostile
    c. Apathetic

25. Willis is a 67 year old man. In addition to memory loss, Willis has problems with language, is disoriented to time and place, misplaces things, is very moody, and has become very passive. Willis may be experiencing:

a. Alzheimer's Disease
b. Grief
c. Depression

SELF-ASSESSMENT:
HOW ANTI-AGING ARE YOU?

Directions: Read each statement. Put a check in the box to reflect whether or not the statement is true or false.

	True	False
I have used whitening toothpaste.		
I have had cosmetic surgery.		
I have had Botox injections.		
I have taken pills to reduce my weight.		
I have taken pills to increase my muscle mass.		
I have taken pills to grow my hair.		
I have taken pills to reduce wrinkles.		
I have used herbal supplements to reduce my weight.		
I have used herbal supplements to increase my muscle mass.		
I have used herbal supplements to grow my hair.		
I have used herbal supplements to reduce wrinkles.		
I have lotions/creams to reduce my weight.		
I have used lotions/creams to increase my muscle mass.		
I have used lotions/creams to grow my hair.		
I have used lotions/creams to reduce wrinkles.		
I have adopted a fad diet that reverses the aging process.		
I have used beverages that reverse the aging process.		
I have read books to learn how to mask aging.		
I have visited websites to learn about masking aging.		
I have purchased videos to learn about masking aging		
I have used make-up to mask aging.		
I exercise in an effort to stay young.		
I have dyed my hair to cover up graying.		
I have hired a professional to test my aging rate.		

Key: Give yourself 1 point for every statement that you checked as 'True.' A score of 24 represents the person with strong anti-aging attitudes. A score of 0 represents the person who is comfortable with aging.

ANSWERS

KEY TERMS CROSSWORD PUZZLE

Across	Page Numbers
7. Thanatologist	536
14. Mourning	534
15. Intimate	531
16. Sandwich	537
17. Social Security	522

Down

1. Surrogate	527
2. Apathetic	531
3. Dementia	518
4. Depression	517
5. Gerontologist	514
6. Retirement	522
8. Life expectancy	514
9. Grief	534
10. Young-old	515
11. Ageism	520
12. Denial	532
13. Congenial	531

POST-TEST

Answers	Page Numbers
1. B	527
2. A	517
3. B	515
4. B	527
5. C	515
6. A	522
7. A	527
8. A	534
9. B	514
10. C	531
11. B	539
12. B	531
13. A	532
14. A	520
15. B	526
16. C	522
17. A	514
18. B	526
19. B	531
20. A	529
21. B	537
22. A	531
23. A	536
24. C	531
25. A	518

18

THE FAMILY IN THE TWENTY-FIRST CENTURY

CHAPTER OBJECTIVES

Upon reading Chapter Eighteen, students should be able to:

1.   Describe variations in family structure in the twenty-first century.

2.   Discuss the racial-ethnic diversity of twenty-first century families.

3.   Explain changes in children's well-being during the twenty-first century.

4.   Discuss family policy in the twenty-first century.

5.   Describe the health patterns of twenty-first century families.

6.   Discuss the economic concerns of twenty-first century families.

7.   Describe global aging in the twenty-first century.

CHAPTER OVERVIEW

Variations in family structures will increase in number and form. There may be more multi-generational households. Senior citizens will depend more on step-kin, and more families may be headed by gays and lesbians. Racial-ethnic diversity will increase. Minorities will make a larger impact on political, educational, and economic institutions. Racial-ethnic communities will continue to grow. Children have been called "the new poor" because poverty rates among children have increased. Almost 12 percent of children living below the poverty level experience "moderate" or "severe" hunger on a daily basis

Family policy, or measures taken by governmental bodies to achieve specific objectives relating to the well-being of families, has improved many children's lives. The first federal law to enforce child-support payment was enacted in 1950. The *1975 Office of Child Support Enforcement Law* created the bureaucracy to enforce private child support obligations. *The 1984 Child Support Enforcement Amendments* required all states to 1) establish child-support enforcement offices, 2) adopt formulas to determine child-support obligations, 3) withhold pay from the wages of delinquent, non-custodial parents, and 4) receive federal reimbursement for about 75% of each state's enforcement costs. *The 1988 Family Support Act* 1) required that judges provide a written justification to depart from state guidelines, 2) instructed states to review and update child-support awards at least every three years, and 3) mandated that states withhold funds for child-support in all cases.

Courts increasingly recognize children's rights. In 35 states, trial judges are required to consider the presence or absence of domestic violence in child-custody disputes. Still, the U.S. is less progressive than other major Western countries. Few U.S. families can afford high-quality child care services while many other countries (Belgium, Italy, and Denmark) provide state-funded schooling programs. Even more, few U.S. companies provide any kind of child-care assistance.

Many countries have developed policies to help employed parents balance work and family responsibilities. In more than 30 developing countries, such as Angola and Ghana, parents can take paid infant-care leave. In the U.S, the 1993 Family and Medical Leave Act provides only unpaid leave and only to some employees. Many developed nations provide generous parental leave benefits. Due to the lack of good child care facilities and an increased number of women entering the work-force or higher education, battles over who should care for children will probably escalate.

Americans are healthier than in the past. Yet, unequal health care and the lack of a national healthcare system will continue to impact the health of families. Health and healthcare vary by race-ethnicity, social class, and geographic area. Minorities suffer with more disabilities and receive lower quality care. The higher one's socio-economic status, the better one's health and healthcare. The U.S. is one of the few industrialized countries that has neither national health insurance nor a system that makes health care a right of all citizens. Despite government programs like Medicaid and Medicare, 24% of the poor have no health insurance. Women are more likely than men to have health insurance. Young people between ages of 18 to 24 are less likely than other age groups to have health insurance. The Canadian healthcare system, which has a publicly funded healthcare, has been considered a model for the U.S. to adopt.

The U.S. has higher child poverty rates than most industrialized countries. One in 5 children in the U.S. lives in poverty. Parents' work is the most important factor in preventing child poverty. One reason for high poverty rates in the U.S. is that the government has failed to adopt a comprehensive antipoverty agenda, such as a living wage. **Welfare** is government aid to people who cannot support themselves, generally because they are unemployed or poor. There are also welfare programs to benefit the middle class, the upper class, and corporations like student loans, farm subsidies, and loans to veterans. The *Personal Responsibility and Work Opportunity Reconciliation Act* (*PRWORA*) or *Welfare Reform Act* eliminated *AFDC* (*Aid to Families with Dependent Children*) and replaced it with *TANF* (*Temporary Aid to Needy Families*), providing a five year limit on welfare benefits. With TANF, recipients must work, enroll in job training, or do community service after two years of receiving benefits. Since 1996, the number of welfare recipients has decreased. Because of welfare reform, there are fewer children in single-parent families and more living with cohabiting families. The cost of *corporate welfare* is greater than that of assistance to poor families. One form of corporate welfare is the Market Access Program, which gives companies money to promote their goods overseas.

The sex gap in pay is the result of employment discrimination and has a negative impact on family. The concept of comparable worth suggests that men and women should receive equal pay for doing equal work. Some states have implemented pay equity laws. Unlike Canada, there is no law that requires private business industry to have pay equity.

The percentage of older people is important to any society because older people depend on government and family for support. *Support ratios*, or *dependency ratios*, present a broad view of the relative size of working and dependent age groups. The **older support ratio** is the number of people age 65 and over per 100 people ages 20 to 64. Many older adults turn to physician-assisted suicide (PAS). In Oregon, the Death with Dignity law legalized doctor-aided suicide. The debate for the right to die was triggered in 1990 when Jack Kevorkian built a 'suicide machine' to help people with chronic pain kill themselves. There has been widespread interest in **living wills**, legal documents in which people can specify which, if any, life support measures they want in case of serious illness and whether or when they want to have such measures discontinued.

The older population is politically strong. AARP is one of the strongest advocates for the elderly. The elderly has the lowest poverty rate in the U.S. As the elderly population grows and life expectancy increases, many elderly will need long-term care. The competition for scarce resources between the young and old may be reduced by increasing the age at which one becomes eligible for benefits.

PRE-TEST

1. When he divorced, Eugene worked in a minimum wage job. Now, Eugene has a job making about $77,000 per year. Eugene's ex-wife is happy that the child-support award that she receives will be reviewed and updated every 3 years, so that she can get a child support raise based on Eugene's increase. Which legislation mandates reviews and updates for child support awards?
    a. Office of Child Support Enforcement Law
    b. Child Support Enforcement Amendment
    c. Family Support Act

2. The year is 1996 and Joyce has been receiving welfare benefits for 16 years. Because of welfare reform, Joyce's benefits from Aid to Families with Dependent Children (AFDC) have been replaced by:
    a. Temporary Assistance to Needy Families
    b. Earned Income Tax Credits
    c. Corporate Welfare

3. The majority of voters in Oregon support the Death with Dignity law. These voters support:
    a. Living wills
    b. Physician-assisted suicide
    c. Social security

4. Agnes grew up in a poor family and she does not want her children to be poor. She does research and finds that the single most important factor in predicting whether children will be poor is:
    a. Race
    b. Parents' work
    c. Parents' divorce

5. Leslie told her mother that she wants to work in the welfare office when she grows up so that she can help the poor. Leslie's mother is concerned about her daughter's career choice because:
    a. The number of people on welfare has declined
    b. The number of people on welfare has increased
    c. The number of people on welfare has remained the same

6. Marian is a poor mother. She receives government aid because she cannot support herself and her children. This aid is called:
    a. Welfare
    b. PAS
    c. Child support

7. Before dying, Emmit created a legal document to specify that he did not want life support in the event of serious illness. This illustrates:
   a. Dying with Dignity
   b. Physician assisted suicide
   c. A living will

8. Marcia believes that men and women should get paid the same amount of money for doing the same job. Marcia is for:
   a. Gender gaps
   b. Comparable worth
   c. Sexism

9. In the U.S., there are 21 persons aged 65 and over for every 100 working-aged persons. This illustrates the:
   a. Older support ratio
   b. Wage gap
   c. Living will ratio

10. Seven-year-old Jenny learned in school about a model health care system that provides heath care to all of its residents. The system most cited as the model for the U.S. is that of:
    a. Canada
    b. Britain
    c. Cuba

11. The U.S. government gave Campbell Soup financial aid to help them promote their canned goods overseas. This illustrates:
    a. The Market Access Program
    b. Corporate Welfare
    c. Both a & b

12. Demographers have noted that welfare reform has impacted family structure. More children are now living with:
    a. Single parent mothers
    b. Cohabiting families
    c. Both a & b

13. Eleanor is running for office in the organization that is the most powerful advocate for the elderly. She is seeking position in the:
    a. NAACP
    b. NOW
    c. AARP

14. Willie has been receiving welfare benefits through Temporary Aid to Needy Families. Under this program, cash assistance cannot exceed ____ years.
    a. 2
    b. 5
    c. 10
    d. 15

15. In his graduation speech, Mike tells his classmates to focus on saving "the new poor" through charity, community service, and political activism. Mike is encouraging his classmates to help:
    a. Immigrants
    b. Children
    c. The elderly

16. The year is 2030. Most of the elderly residents of Shady Pines Nursing home depend on step-kin as much as biological relatives. This is the result of a high number of:
    a. Physician assisted suicide
    b. Dependency ratios
    c. Divorces and remarriages

17. Leslie believes that the future of America is threatened by the fact that 1 out of every ____ children live in poverty.
    a. 3
    b. 5
    c. 10
    d. 100

18. This semester in Law School, Ahmad learned about Child Support Enforcement Act and The Family and Medical Leave Act. These measures taken by the government for the well-being of families is called:
    a. Family policy
    b. Welfare reform
    c. Both a & b

19. Saleem is a 42 year old man. Nabeel is a 22 year old man. Which man is least likely to have health insurance?
    a. Saleem
    b. Nabeel
    c. They are equally likely

20. Renee was just hired as a Child Enforcement Officer. The legislation that created the bureaucracy that Renee works for is called the:
    a. Office of Child Support Enforcement Law
    b. Child Support Enforcement Amendment
    c. Family Support Act

21. Bhummi is an accountant. She plans to take time off from work to care for her newborn bay. Bhummi is horrified to learn that although the company that she works for will allow her time off, the time off is unpaid. Which legislation provides for unpaid leave?
    a. The Family & Medical Leave Act
    b. The Family Support Act
    c. The Market Access Program

22. Children's rights advocates believe that trial judges should consider whether there is domestic violence when assigning child-custody. In the U.S., ____ states mandate such considerations.
    a. 15
    b. 25
    c. 35

23. Michelle was surprised to learn that developing countries provided services to citizens that the U.S. does not provide its residents. Developing countries that offer paid infant-care leave include:
    a. Angola
    b. Ghana
    c. Both a & b

24. Skylar is poor. Nastaja is middle class. Who is more likely to be sick?
    a. Skylar
    b. Nastaja
    c. They are equally likely

25. The year is 1988, and Kevin is delinquent in his child support payments. Which legislation requires states to withhold a part of Kevin's pay check for child support payments?
    a. Office of Child Support Enforcement Law
    b. Child Support Enforcement Amendment
    c. Family Support Act

EXERCISES/APPLICATIONS

1. More governmental welfare funds are used for corporations than for families. How do you feel that welfare funds should be divided between the poor; the middle class, the upper class, and the government? Explain your preference.

2. The wage gap between women and men stems from, among other things, employment discrimination. Is *comparable worth* a realistic goal by the first part of the next century? Why or why not?

CHAPTER 18 KEY TERMS CROSSWORD PUZZLE

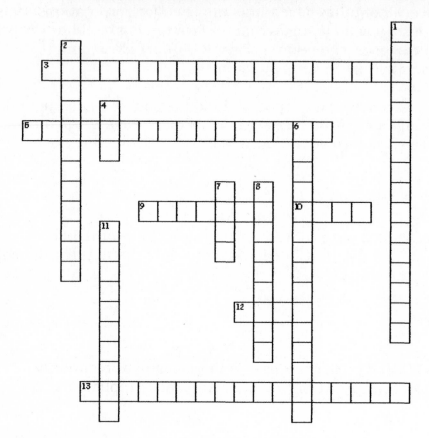

Across

3. Government aid to promote overseas sales
5. Common name for PRWORA
9. Government aid to the needy
10. Advocate for the elderly
12. One in ___ U.S. children live in poverty
13. # of people 65+ per 100 people 20-64

Down

1. Enacted in 1988
2. Government efforts to improve kin groups
4. Doctor supported death
6. Equal pay for equal work
7. Replaced AFDC
8. Suicide machine creator
11. Legal document specifying dying instructions

POST-TEST

1. The year is 2025 and Pedro, a Latino politician, wants to run for senate. His campaign manager tells him that it is best to move to a state where there is a larger number of Latinos. Pedro should move to:
   a. Pennsylvania
   b. Texas
   c. Wisconsin

2. Leroy is a black six year old. Spike is a white six year old. Which child is more likely to suffer with disabilities?
   a. Leroy
   b. Spike
   c. They are equally likely

3. Amanda works as a caseworker in the state's Office of Public Assistance. Since the 1996 Welfare Reform Act, the number of people receiving welfare benefits has:
   a. Increased
   b. Decreased
   c. Remained the same

4. The year is 2020. The teacher asks Ana how large the minority population in the United States is. Ana correctly replies:
   a. 10%
   b. 20%
   c. 30%

5. Researchers suggest that by the year 2030, there will be 36 people aged 65 and over for every 100 working age people. This illustrates the future:
   a. Living will ratio
   b. Wage gap
   c. Older support ratio

6. Wanda is a woman living in Chicago. Lucious is a man living in Chicago. Who is more likely to have health insurance?
   a. Wanda
   b. Lucuios
   c. They are equally likely

7. The economic position of the elderly has changed. They now have the _____ poverty rate in the U.S.
   a. Highest
   b. Lowest
   c. Neither a nor b

8. As she prepares for her run for president of the United States, the candidate often makes reference to the healthcare system that is most applauded as the one that Americans should adopt. The healthcare system often cited as the 'model' is:
   a. Britain
   b. Cuba
   c. Canada

9. Three years ago, Raymond divorced his wife. Since then, he has had to pay $250 per month in child support. This month, a judge will review and update the amount that Raymond contributes to his children. Which legislation mandates such reviews?
   a. Office of Child Support Enforcement Law
   b. Child Support Enforcement Amendment
   c. Family Support Act

10. Pauline completes a social studies project on lessening the competition for scarce resources between the young and the elderly. She suggests that the age at which one becomes eligible for old-age benefits should:
    a. Be lowered
    b. Be raised
    c. Remain the same

11. Terrell tells his business partners that the men and women working in their company should be paid the same amount of money for doing the same job. Terrell supports:
    a. Sex discrimination
    b. Gender gaps
    c. Comparable worth

12. Today, Willie and his classmates learned about the man who created the suicide machine in 1990. The creator was:
    a. Bill Clinton
    b. Jack Kevorkian
    c. Pat Schroeder

13. Lorraine studies child care provisions around the world. She notes that 60% of child care in _____ is provided by the government.
    a. Japan
    b. United States
    c. Canada

14. Inez is an economic analyst. She appears on the news to inform the public that "the new poor" in America are:
    a. Children
    b. The elderly
    c. White men

15. Minnie and Mickey are debating about the cost of welfare. Minnie believes that the government gives more money to the poor. Mickey believes that the government gives more money to corporations. Who is correct?
    a. Minnie
    b. Mickey
    c. Neither - there is no difference in the amounts provided to the poor and corporations

16. Shanna is a British woman with a Master's degree in Business Administration. She is more skilled than all of the men in her graduating class. Yet, all of the job offers that she has received offer her less than her male counterparts. Shanna is moving to the place where gender equity laws are most common. Shanna will move to:
    a. Mexico
    b. U.S.A.
    c. Canada

17. Elise receives governmental aid to raise her 6 children. Elise is about to be removed from the welfare rolls because she has reached her lifetime limit. The lifetime limit of welfare benefits is:
    a. 2 years
    b. 5 years
    c. 10 years
    d. 15 years

18. Oregon's Death with Dignity Act is concerned with:
    a. Physician assisted suicide
    b. Living wills
    c. Social Security

19. The year is 2025. Nicola and Fernando are migrating to America from South America. They want to live in a state with a large number of Latinos. The couple should move to:
    a. California
    b. Utah
    c. Oregon

20. The year is 1984, and Stephanie has not received a child-support
payment from her ex-husband in 4 years. Stephanie is happy to hear
that new legislation requires states to withhold a part of ex-husband's
pay check for child support payments. The legislation is called:
    a. Office of Child Support Enforcement Law
    b. Child Support Enforcement Amendment
    c. Family Support Act

21. As a teacher in a poor neighborhood, Heather is not surprised to
learn that 1 out of every ___ children in the U.S. lives in poverty.
    a. 3
    b. 5
    c. 10
    d. 100

22. The man running for governor of the state promises voters that he
will eliminate child poverty. The candidate will have to address the
most important predictor of child poverty which is:
    a. Race
    b. Parents' work
    c. Parents' divorce

23. The year is 1996, and Thomasina's welfare benefits have just been
cut. This cut is the result of the:
    a. Welfare Reform Act
    b. Market Access Program
    c. Aid to Families with Dependent Children

24. Angela wants to go to Washington D.C. to shape governmental
actions in an effort to improve family well-being. Angela wants to
contribute to:
    a. Welfare
    b. Family leave
    c. Family policy

25. Demographers have noted that welfare reform has impacted family
structure. Fewer children are now living with:
    a. Single parent mothers
    b. Cohabiting families
    c. Both a & b

SELF-ASSESSMENT:
HOW CONTENT ARE YOU WITH FAMILY LIFE IN THE 21st CENTURY?

Directions: Read each statement. Put a check in the box to reflect whether or not you agree.

	Agree	Disagree
Societies benefit when minorities have more political power.		
It is better for people to live alone than in families.		
Society benefits when fewer couples have children.		
Gays and lesbians should have more rights.		
Non-custodial parents should be forced to pay child support.		
Parents, not the government, should furnish child care for children.		
It is not the government's responsibility to provide paid parental leave for American parents.		
The government should not sponsor a national health care system.		
The best way to get people off of welfare is to require them to work.		
Businesses should receive more assistance from the government than the poor.		
Men should be paid more than women.		
It is good for minorities to have more economic power.		
Assisted-suicide should be legalized across the nation.		
The age at which people qualify for elderly benefits should be raised.		
It is good that the minority population is increasing.		

Key: Give yourself 1 point for every statement that you checked as 'Agree.' A score of 15 represents the person who is most content with the 21st century family. A score of 0 represents the person who is least content. Use this information to fuel your political involvement.

ANSWERS

PRE-TEST

Answers	Page Numbers
1. C	547
2. A	552
3. B	555
4. B	551
5. A	552
6. A	552
7. C	556
8. B	534
9. A	554
10. A	550
11. B	553
12. B	553
13. C	556
14. B	552
15. B	547
16. C	546
17. B	551
18. A	547
19. B	549
20. A	547
21. A	548
22. C	547
23. C	548
24. A	549
25. B	547

KEY TERMS CROSSWORD PUZZLE

Across	Page Numbers
3. Market Access Program	553
5. Welfare Reform Act	552
9. Welfare	552
10. AARP	556
12. Five	551
13. Older support ratio	554

Down	
1. Family Support Act	547
2. Family policy	547
4. Physician Assisted Suicide	555
6. Comparable worth	534
7. TANF	552
8. Kevorkian	555
11. Living Will	556

POST-TEST

Answers	Page Numbers
1. B	546
2. A	549

3. B	552
4. C	546
5. C	554
6. A	549
7. B	556
8. C	550
9. B	547
10. B	557
11. C	534
12. B	555
13. A	548
14. A	547
15. B	533
16. C	554
17. B	552
18. A	556
19. A	546
20. B	547
21. B	551
22. B	551
23. A	552
24. C	548
25. A	553